MEXICO'S
Copper Canyon
Barranca del Cobre

By
Richard D. Fisher
Luis G. Verplancken, S.J.
Kit Williams
Carlos Lazcano
and
Jonathan E. "Jack" Davis
Silvia Marinas-Feliner
Spencer Heath MacCallum
Walter P. Parks
www.coppercanyon.org
www.canyonsworldwide.com
www.great-adventures.com

THE GOVERNOR OF THE STATE OF CHIHUAHUA

C.P. Patricio Martinez Garcia
Gobernador Constitucional del Estado de Chihuahua

Dear Reader,

Chihuahua, a frontier state of high adventure forged in the crucible of the eternal struggle against the natural elements and the challenges of distance, offers those who visit an unforgettable experience. Located in northern Mexico, with an area of 247,087 square kilometers, the state enables visitors to experience natural regions considered unique in the world. Prominent among them are the Sierra Tarahumara, with its imposing canyons, and the desert, with beauty simultaneously serene and wild.

Chihuahua's grandeur derives not only from the size of its territory, its natural ecology, or the variety of its landscape; these features nurture and increase the richness of its historical legacy, its living cultures, and the warmth of its people.

The mountainous region—where forested country contrasts with the tropical vegetation of the canyons—is the land of the Tarahumara culture. Today they still preserve their centuries-old traditions and customs. There, the Jesuit missionaries of the sixteenth, seventeenth, and eighteenth centuries traveled to extend the European way of life to these deeply hidden places, leaving for posterity clear footprints of their passage.

On the vast plains the Paquime culture developed from the tenth to fourteenth centuries, which with its enormous buildings and irrigation works brought life to the Casas Grandes Valley. The Museo de las Culturas del Norte (museum of northern cultures), located in the archaeological zone (and recently declared a World Heritage Site by UNESCO), testifies to this culture, as well as the intense trading between it and the towns in what is now the American Southwest.

Mining settlements such as Parral, Santa Barbara, and San Francisco del Oro, located in the southern part of the state, possess the characteristic seal of consolidation of the Spanish advance. Meriting special mention is the Allende Valley, a vineyard with a strong colonial legacy and characteristic architecture of the late sixteenth and early seventeenth centuries.

This brief description barely begins to show that which is Chihuahua. It is a place where tourists may enjoy geography, history, and culture, and where visitors are welcomed and treated with the characteristic hospitality that distinguishes Chihuahuans.

Estimado Lector,

Chihuahua, estado de avanzada y aventura, forjado en el crisol de la eterna lucha en contra de los elementos naturales y la adversidad de la distancia, ofrece a quienes la visitan una experiencia inolvidable. Situado al norte de Mexico, sus 247,087 kilómentros cuadrados de territorio le permiten contar con regiones naturales consideradas de características unicas en el mundo. Destacan entre ellas, la Sierra Tarahumara con sus imponentes barrancas, asi como el desierto, con su belleza serena y bárbara a la vez.

Su grandeza se deriva no solo de la amplitud de su territorio, su universo natural o la variedad del paisaje, sino que se nutre y acrecenta de la riqueza de su legado histórico, de sus culturas vivas y sobre todo, de la calidez de su gente.

En la zona serrana, donde contrasta el paisaje boscoso de la montaña con la vegetación tropical de las barrancas, la geografía cobra sentido con la cultura tarahumara, que aun hoy en dia conserva sus tradiciones y costumbres milenarias. Ahi, los misioneros jesuitas durante los siglos XVI, XVII y XVIII fueron extendiendo la forma de vida europea hasta los mas escondidos parajes, dejando para la posteridad huella clara de su paso.

En la amplitud de la planicie, alrededor de los siglos X al XIV se desarrolló la cultura paquimé, que con sus enormes construcciones y sus obras de irrigación dio vida al valle de Casas Grandes. El Museo de las Culturas del Norte, ubicado en la zona arqueológica (recientemente declarada por la UNESCO como Patrimonio Cultural de la Humanidad), ofrece testimonio de esta cultura, asi como del intenso intercambio que mantuvo con los pueblos del ahora Suroeste norteamericano.

Poblaciones mineras como Parral, Santa Barbara y San Francisco del Oro, que se situan al sur del estado, poseen el sello característico de la consolidación del avance español, mereciendo mencion aparte el Valle de Allende, un vergel con un fuerte legado colonia y muestras de arquitectura de fines del siglo XVI y principios del XVII.

Esta breve descripcion apenas si constituye una muestra de lo que es Chihuahua, lugar donde el turista puede disfrutar ampliamente de la geografía, la historia y la cultura, donde sus visitantes son bienvenidos y tratados con la caraterística hospitalidad que distingue a los chihuahuenses.

Copper Canyon — Barranca del Cobre
Chihuahua, Mexico
By Richard D. Fisher

Contents

SUNRACER PUBLICATIONS
P.O. Box 86492
Tucson, AZ 85754
Phone: (520) 882-5341
Fax: (520) 882-4454
www.coppercanyon.org
www.canyonsworldwide.com

Photography
Richard D. Fisher
Luis G. Verplancken, S.J.
Carlos Lazcano

Text
Richard D. Fisher
Luis G. Verplancken, S.J.
Kit Williams
Jonathan E. "Jack" Davis
Silvia Marinas-Feliner
www.great-adventures.com

Design
Raymond C. Harden

Illustrations
Susan Bigda

Color Production
Hollis Digital Images

Editors
Susan Bigda

Maps
Raymond C. Harden
Nora Voutas

Typesetting
Koala-t Type

Library of Congress Catalog Card Number 89-52202   ISBN Number 0-9619170-6-7

Rails to Adventure

The Chihuahua-Pacífico Railroad was inaugurated in November 1961. This rail line is probably one of the world's finest engineering wonders, with its 39 bridges and 86 tunnels. The line is the only land connection between Los Mochis and Chihuahua City.

Each day one train departs Los Mochis at 6 a.m. bound for Chihuahua while another train departs Chihuahua at 7 a.m. bound for Los Mochis. The trip takes about 12 hours. Overnight stops are permitted at no extra charge. Jet air service is available daily to Los Mochis and Chihuahua via various carriers. Nowhere else on earth can one reach such a wild and ruggedly beautiful region so quickly and comfortably.

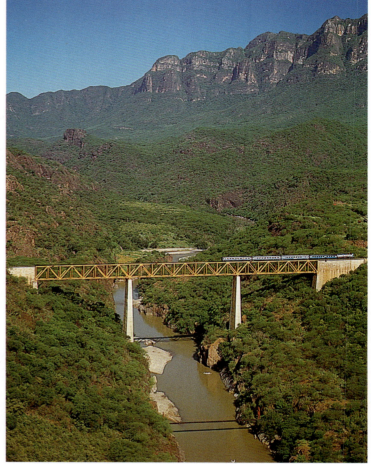

Urique Canyon

Basaseachi Falls

Cueva de la Rancheria

Cueva de la Momia

The Cave Dwellings of
Huapoca Canyon - Madera

These remote pre-Columbian sites and artifacts are fast disappearing. Carlos Lazcano, who provided the first modern insight into this ancient culture and permission to use these rare photographs, is leading the preservation effort as Director of Ecotourism for the state of Chihuahua. His love and appreciation for these "lost worlds" are the driving force for modern preservation and conservation.

Casas Grandes - Mata Ortiz - Cave Valley

On the high plains of Chihuahua, a beautiful Native American civilization flourished seven centuries ago. Called Casas Grandes by the first Spanish explorers, today in this area is dawning a new era of artistic expression based on the ancient art form of ceramics.

The ancients, possibly much like the Tarahumara people of today, had a major cultural center on the river plain with *rancherías* scattered in the high mountains nearby. At least some of the native residents would undoubtedly migrate to these high valleys during the summer months to grow crops.

Called Paquimé and Cave Valley respectively, these two areas now provide respite from modern industrial development as well as an opportunity to learn about pre-Columbian culture. Cueva de la Olla contains one of the most exotic grain storage "jars" anywhere in the New World. The valley in which the cave exists is one of the most beautiful in the northern Sierra Madre.

Mata Ortiz, a small village that springs up unexpectedly from rough cattle country between Casas Grandes and Cave Valley, is a modern phenomenon of innovation in world-class, thin-walled pottery and hand-painted ceramics. Juan Quezada, first discovered in 1976, is the person who bridged the gap from the ancient utilitarian art form of pottery to the modern world's demand for exceedingly high-quality artistic expression that is economically viable. This story of the phoenix of a new culture rising from the ashes of the old is one of the most exciting stories in Mexico today.

Casas Grandes - Mata Ortiz Ceramics

The story behind the pottery tradition begins with the Paquimé (Casas Grandes) ruins. The people who lived at Paquimé between A.D. 1060 and 1340 made intricately painted clay containers. This ancient tradition ended as abruptly as it began lying dormant for a full 700 years.

In the early 1970s Juan Quezada began to experiment with this art form. Ancient pottery shards were abundant in the area. Using the shards and whole vessels dug from the ruins for inspiration, Juan developed his own ceramic technology and style.

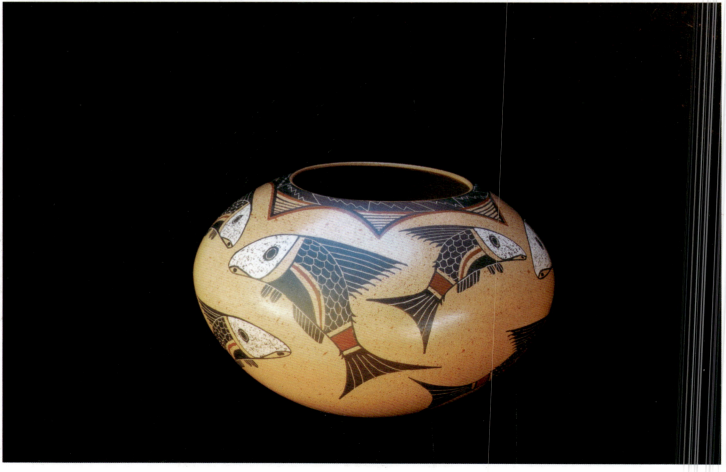

Juan discovered natural clay deposits in the region. Formulas for pigments that could withstand the heat of firing and be permanent were perfected using local mineral and vegetable materials.

Brushes for applying pigments are now made from the potter's own hair. A single strand approximately two inches long is used to apply the fine lines. These lines create the intricate patterns and mazes defining the character of an individual piece.

Each piece is formed using a pinching method. The base begins with a flat tortilla-shaped piece of clay. This piece is laid into a bowl-shaped mold. This mold determines the size of the pot. The clay is then smoothed outward by pressing it into the base. The sides are then pinched upward by hand forming the lower half of the pot. A rope of clay is joined to the outer edge of the form and the pinching, then the turning method continues. Once the basic shape is formed, it is then refined using various tools such as the toothed edge of a hacksaw blade or a piece of rounded tin. This operation takes about two hours.

While the pot is still wet, slip is applied and the design is painted. Painting takes approximately three more hours. Immediately after painting, a thin film of plastic is placed around the pot and rubbed lightly with the polishing stone. This seals the pigments into the clay to prevent smearing when the pot is completely dry and the final polishing is done using a smooth tumbled agate.

At this point the pot is ready for firing. A thin layer of cow chips is ignited and allowed to burn to coals. The bottom of the pot is placed on a small wire rack just above the coals. A wire cage is then placed over the pot and cow chips are built up covering the cage in a beehive fashion. This mound is then ignited and allowed to burn to ashes (approximately twenty-five minutes). When the firing is complete, the cage is removed and the pot is hung to cool. This completes the entire process.

This information provided courtesy of Tito Carrillo a longtime *pochteca* (trader) of Mata Ortiz ceramics. For further information you can contact him at Casa Molina • 6225 E. Speedway • Tucson, Arizona 85712 • (520) 290-0305.

Canyon Tarahumara – Semana Santa

Canyon Tarahumara – Semana Santa

Mountain Tarahumara – Virgin of Guadalupe Festival

Chihuahua
Rails: The New Gateway To The Sierra Madre

In 1872 Albert Kinsey Owen, an American utopian dreamer, first conceived the idea to construct a rail line between Topolobampo Bay in Sinaloa and Kansas City, Kansas. The route would shorten the existing rail route from San Francisco to Kansas City by more than 400 miles.

The rail route opened on November 23, 1961. Incredible physical, political and economic difficulties had to be overcome and it was not until nearly a century later, the last stubborn section of track, which drops 7,000 feet in 122 miles, took over 20 years to complete. This last phase was financed and directed by the Mexican government itself. Many names famous in railroad and international history were involved over the years. Enrique C. Creel, Ulysses S. Grant, Don Porfirio Díaz, Admiral George W. Dewey, Pancho Villa, Arthur Stillwell, Benjamin F. Johnson, C. Adolfo López Mateos, and the Tarahumara Indians all played key roles in making the dream a reality.

It took all the engineering skill that could be mustered after WW II to finish the Sierra and Barrancas sections of the route. The first major engineering feat, namely traveling uphill, is made at the beautiful Témoris Station. The track crosses two curving bridges which reverse the direction of ascent. After crossing the Río Septentrión and a tributary on these bridges, the track ascends by successively higher loops until it disappears into a long tunnel. The second spectacular engineering feat is near the station of Pitorreal, about 40 miles west of Creel. Here the line actually circles back over itself in a complete loop. *This is one of only three examples of this type of railway engineering North America.*

The rail trip from Los Mochis to Chihuahua has 36 major bridges and 87 tunnels, adding excitement to the 300 miles of track, that follow a tortuous route from sea level to a maximum elevation of more than 8,000 feet at its highest point.

It is best to begin your tour at Los Mochis, as the most spectacular section of the ride, between the Témoris and Creel Stations, should always be seen in the daylight. Often the downhill run is late and passes through these incredibly scenic canyons after dark.

Leaving Los Mochis about dawn, the train passes through the Sinaloan Thornforest life zone. This area is characterized as a cactus and thorntree jungle, and is very exotic in appearance. At the Agua Caliente station, the train passes over the Río Fuerte on a large bridge and enters the foothills of the Sierra. At this point the track begins to climb more sharply.

Shortly after entering the foothills, the train crosses the spectacularly beautiful high bridge over the Chínipas River. Be sure to look down as you cross this trestle and see the foot and burro bridge suspended above the river, hundreds of feet below.

Following the Chínipas bridge, the train begins to pass through numerous tunnels and enters true canyon country. In Río Septentrión Canyon you canlook down on many beautiful pools and cascades in the river below. Here the environment is tropical and lush with palm, banana, and mango trees. At Témoris Station the track bridges the river, climbs through a great loop, and enters a tunnel. You'll observe a complete change in environment upon emerging from the tunnels on the elevated side of this big "jump." This upper canyon has a distinctive alpine feeling, with the surrounding forest being predominately oak and pine.

The train continues to climb steeply through the canyon as it reaches the Divisadero overlook. You will feel a definite nip in the air as you disembark for about 10 minutes to get a brief look at Copper Canyon. The track continues to climb after Divisadero, but the surrounding environment changes from canyon to mountain. Vast forested mountains and ridges spanvistas of up to 100 miles.

Between Creel and La Junta, the track continues through the mountain environment interspersed by beautiful valleys, each with its own picturesque village.

At La Junta, the train descends to the plains of Chihuahua. These beautiful grassy plains are interrupted by isolated mountain ranges and Mennonite farms. Sit back and savor the scenery of this peaceful area, as you recover from the excitement of the canyons now fading into the sunset.

It is astonishing that the trip from Los Mochis to Chihuahua can be made in one day. On the "Choo-Choo to Chihuahua," as a friend of mine affectionately calls this trip, you'll enjoy some of the most spectacular scenery on earth in the comfort of a modern railway coach. It is truly one of the most exciting excursions available to people of all ages anywhere in the world.

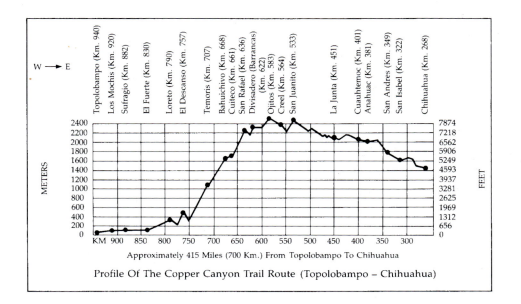

Profile Of The Copper Canyon Trail Route (Topolobampo – Chihuahua)

Railroad Log of Major Points of Interest
Los Mochis - Chihuahua

When using this log, watch for the kilometer posts beside the track. Each tunnel is also numbered on the righthand side as the train enters.

941.0km *Topolobampo.* After he saw the large natural harbor at Topolobampo, Albert K. Owen's project to establish autopian agricultural colony assured the dimensions of a dream. He visualized a great international seaport for commerce between the Pacific Basin and the United States. The seaport would be linked to the mid-western United States by rail across the rugged Sierra Madre Occidental of Mexico. The railroad would shorten by 400 miles the distance between Kansas City and the Pacific.

920.4km *Los Mochis,* whose name means "place of turtles" in the Mayo Indian language, is about 20 miles to the west of Topolobampo. Los Mochis was founded in 1903 by an American, Benjamin Johnson, who established large sugar plantations and a sugar mill. Today, more than 300,000 hectares (750,000 acres) are cultivated with crops including sugarcane, alfalfa, cotton, rice, and winter vegetables.

882.0km *San Blas (Sufragio) Station.* Elevation: 105 feet. At San Blas, the Ferrocarril Chihuahua al Pacífico crosses the Ferrocarril Pacífico, which extends from Nogales to Guadalajara.

838.6 km *El Fuerte* was established late in the sixteenth century, when the viceroy of New Spain (Mexico) ordered the construction of a fort to protect settlers from the attacks of rebellious Indians. Also located here is a fine Balderrama family hotel.

781.0 km *Bridge over the Rio Fuerte.* This bridge is 1,637 feet in length, the longest on the railroad. Have your camera ready.

780.0 km *Agua Caliente* village and railroad station.

754.0 km This bridge, spanning the Río Chínipas, is the highest bridge on the railway at 355 feet above the river and 1,000 feet in length. On your right toward the south you will see a suspension bridge for foot traffic. It's called the Chinípas Foot Bridge.

739.0 km Tunnels #79-82. These tunnels range between 124 and 780 feet in length.

736.0 km *Santo Niño.* A little railroad camp and siding. Most of the boxcars are ex-WW II troop cars now serving as homes for the railroad workers.

722.4 km Tunnels #71-78. These range from 65 to 581 feet in length.

721.0 km Tunnels #66-70, ranging from 305 to 639 feet in length.

718.0km To the left is one of the steepest cornfields in the world. Trees and vegetation have been burned off.

717.0 km Tunnels #64 (880 feet) and #65 (450 feet).

711.0 km Tunnels #53-63. The lengths of these tunnels range between 139 and 657 feet.

710.8 km Mina Plata Bridge (348 feet).

710.4 km Tunnel #52 (1,023 feet).

710.0 km Tunnel #51 (1,143 feet).

709.0 km Tunnel #50 (413 feet).

707.1 km As we approach Témoris (elev. 3,365 feet), the railway crosses the *Santa Bárbara Bridge* (714 feet) over the Río Mina Plata, a tributary of the Río Septentrión. The Río Septentrión and Río Chínipas, join to become the Río Fuerte. Mexican rivers are not named in the same manner as in the United States so this system is often confusing to us.

707.0km The village of *Témoris* is located on a plateau high above the station. The village was founded in 1677 by two Jesuit missionaries, who named it Santa María Magdalena de Témoris. Témoris was the name of a tribe of Indians who inhabited the region.

704.8 km Tunnel #49, known as the La Pera, is 3,074 feet in length.

704.0 km The commemorative marker built for the dedication of the railroad by President López Mateos on November 24, 1961, is constructed of rails 22 feet long with letters 2 feet high. Here are views of the railroad descending by means of curves and loops. At one point, three levels of railroad are visible. Also in view is tunnel #49 and the spectacular twin waterfall.

703.0 km Tunnels #48 (623 feet) and #47 (115 feet).

701.0 km Tunnels #46 (2,680 feet), #45 (662 feet), #44 (479 feet), and #43 (384 feet).

695.8km Between kilometer posts 695.8 and 662.6, are many bridges and tunnels, ranging in length from 220 to 1,102 feet.

668.1 km *Bahuichivo.* Get off here for Cerocahui, the Hotel Mission, and Urique Canyon.

662.0 km *Cuiteco,* an interesting little village with a church and numerous old buildings, was originally an Indian village. A mission was established here in 1684 by the noted Jesuit missionary Padre Salvatierra. "Cuiteco" is derived from a Tarahumara word meaning "neck-shaped hill." The area is noted for the production of apples. Many orchards may be seen in the valley and on the slopes.

656.8km From kilometer posts 656.8 through 649, there are again many tunnels.

640.8km Between kilometer posts 640.8 and 638.3 the tunnels range from 351 to 1,512 feet in length.

633.0 km Tunnels #16 (180 feet) and #15 (369 feet).

626.0 km *Posada Barrancas Hotel.* Fine accommodations by the Balderrama family.

623.0 km Tunnel #14 (377 feet).

622.0km *Divisadero* overlooks a tributary of the Río Urique in the Barranca del Cobre. You may also reach Divisadero by walking about an hour from Posada Barrancas. It is the first dramatic view of the canyon.

601.8km *Pitorreal*

585.0 km *El Lazo* (The Loop) is an incredible turn where the rail actually crosses over itself

583.0km Highest point on the railroad: 8,071 feet.

575.0km *El Balcón View.*

563.8km *Creel* is a lumber town of about 5,000 people, nestled in the mountains away from the edge of the canyon. Creel was named after Enrique Creel, governor of Chihuahua, who with Arthur Stillwell in the late 1890s promoted the original Kansas City, Mexico, and Orient Railroad. Life in Creel centers around the lumbering operations, the railroad, the Jesuit Hospital of Fr. Verplancken which treats the Tarahumara Indians, and the tourists who come and go. You will be very interested in the Mission Store. This store buys from the Indians all year long and resells to visitors. The proceeds help offset the operating expenses of the 75-bed hospital.

650.1km *La Mora Bridge,* 445 feet in length.

555.0km *Bocoyna.* was founded in 1702 by Jesuit Missionaries as Nuestra Señora de Guadalupe de Bocoyna. The name means "pine-forest" in Tarahumara.

531.0km *San Juanito,* 8,000 feet above sea level, was established with the arrival of the railroad in 1906. Its temperatures are the coldest of any town in Mexico.

534.0km Bridge over Arroyo Ancho.

461.0km *Miñaca,* a small settlement whose name is a corruption of the Tarahumara word "muguyaca," meaning mountain lion.

471.0km Bridge over Río San Pedro.

451.0km *La Junta Station,* located 6,775 feet above sea level, is the roundhouse for the railroad and a major railroad junction. One track branches north from here to Ciudad Juárez. The river we will cross before La Junta is a tributary to the Río Papigochic, which joins the Río Aros in Sonora and empties into the Gulf of California.

400.0km *Cuauhtémoc.* The village grew with the arrival of the railroad in 1900 but was accelerated with the arrival of the Mennonites in 1921-1922. In 1927 the name was changed in honor of the last Aztec emperor (Cuauhtémoc).

346.3 km Tunnel #2 (367 feet).

349.0km *San Andrés Station.* This village was founded in 1696 by Franciscan missionaries and named San Andrés de Osaguiqui. In 1932 the name was changed to Riva Palacios in honor of General Vicente Palacios, a writer and hero of the war against the French.

319.0km After crossing the highway, the train enters the village *General Trías,* founded by Franciscan missionaries in 1668 and named Santa Isabel de Tarahumaras. In 1932 the village was renamed in honor of General Angel Trías, a hero who successfully expelled the French from México in 1862-1863.

268.0km *Chihuahua City.* Capital of Chihuahua, the largest state in México.

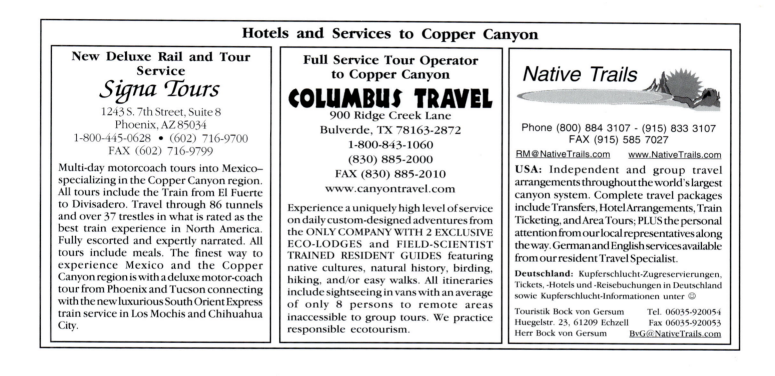

Cerocahui Mission

Cuzarare Mission

The Rarámuri Or Tarahumaras
by Luis G. Verplancken, S.J.

This brief essay does not pretend to be an anthropological monograph as regards the Tarahumara culture: there are many such studies, some of which are quite good. There are also studies about specific aspects of this culture, such as its economy, the footrace in which a wooden ball is used, the batari (ritual drink of the Rarámuri), etc. This is simply an essay based on my day-to-day experiences after having lived for 37 years in an almost uninterrupted manner among these noble peoples who are loyal to God, to their traditions, and to their culture.

Given the length of this essay, what is set down here is but a sketch touching on some of the more important aspects of Tarahumara culture, their rites and customs: it is quite impossible to do justice to a culture as rich as this in just a few pages.

I will attempt to bring together some data which is of interest to the public at large and about which I am questioned with some frequency. These data relate generally to the native culture of the Tarahumara, and touch as well on other interesting cultural aspects not so well known; e.g., their philosophy of life and their way of interrelating with God, with man, and with their community. I will refer to them as the Rarámuri "The People" – as they refer to themselves ("Tarahumara" is only a corruption of the word Rarámuri: Taramuri, inverted as Tarumari, thus, Tarahumara).

I will speak to what we could call a common denominator – the Rarámuri Pagótuame (people who have been baptized) – and not to a particular geographical location, nor to the "gentile" or non-Christian Rarámuri (of which there exist some groups). It is about these Rarámuri Pagótuame, among whom I have had the privilege of living, that I write.

The Ancestors Of The Rarámuri

"The Tarahumara Indians, ancestors probably came from Asia by way of the Bering Strait sometime between fifteen and twenty thousand years ago. Their culture at the time was late Paleolithic or possibly early Neolithic. These migrants from Asia were of Mongoloid stock. They were hunters and gatherers. Their agricultural development was a major technological advancement. Maize or Indian corn, developed in Central or South America back in pre-history, revolutionized their lives. Thousands of years of social striving left them intensity of life, a form of life, a beauty in human relationship, a happiness and an amplitude of personality which the modern world today probably lacks despite its superior technological evolution.

"Closer to our times, perhaps early in the Christian era, they descended with the Aztecs who settled further south. They have remained, even to this day, among the most compact and unmixed of any of the Indian tribes of Mexico. The men are swarthy and stalwart, fleet of foot and strong of limb." (Collier, John: *Indians of the Americas,* pp. 17-20, The New American Library, New York, 1947.)

Dress

The typical dress of the Rarámuri, who are perhaps the most primitive peoples as yet untouched by modem Mexican civilization, consists, for the male, of a breechcloth commonly known as the *tagora,* which is held together by a wool girdle wrapped twice around the waist; the *koyera,* a cloth band worn around the temples to keep the hair in place; the *napatza,* a loose, full-sleeved shirt of cotton, and sandals, *akaka,* on the feet. These last were formerly made of hide. Today they are commonly made of rubber tire soles and leather thong ties. This typical dress is disappearing in many areas of the Sierra Tarahumara. It is in the manner of dress that civilization has had its greatest impact, particularly among the men. The women are more conservative and more resistant to change. Great weight is given to the opinion of other women; a "what will they say" attitude prevails.

The women wear the *siputza or sipucba,* multiple or layered full skirts which are cinched around the waist and gathered horizontally at the mid-thigh and hem. Nonflammable cotton is the material of choice for the skirts. Bright colors, particularly red, and patterned cloth are favored, but it is not unusual for skirts to be made of bleached cotton. The blouses are always worn loose at the waist. They have full sleeves which reach a little below the elbow, and which are heavily pleated at the shoulders and wrists. Like the men, the women use the koyera, or they sometimes use a bandana to cover the head. This is knotted either at the chin or behind the head, depending on the custom of the area.

In some places the use of the koyera has disappeared: the men wear a hat, and the women wear the bandana. The color of the koyera has no particular significance as some have stated. However, for festive wear, a koyera of bright or showy colors is preferred. Women also use the *gimira,* a shawl which is very useful for carrying a child or objects on the back. The *teivekes,* or little girls, dress exactly like their mothers. They learn from a very early age to carry their little brothers or objects on their back with the gimira. Women, too, wear huaraches, but it is common to see both women and young children go barefoot in some places.

Experiences Born Of Sorrow

The culture of the Rarámuri cannot be understood without referring to their history, which has necessarily influenced their lives, customs, and habitat. Their communal experience of the past few centuries is most important in trying to understand some aspects of their lives today and of their attitude toward the white man, whose victim they have always been. From the time of the very first excursions into their territory by miners seeking gold and silver, they were forced to work in the mines and were treated as slaves. Their best lands were taken from them, and they were considered to be uncouth pariahs. As a conquered people, they had no rights and were expected to bend to the will of their new masters. Although military force was used to subjugate them, they rebelled from time to time. They suffered wholesale massacres during the campaigns to dominate them, and this brought about certain attitudinal changes. Some opted to retreat to more remote sites where they could live in peace, although this meant giving up their best lands. Others opted for a strategy of peaceful resistance, even though it was very distasteful for them to work in the mines; this entailed penetrating into the bowels of the earth, near the place where *reré beteáme,* He Who Lives Below, is found – in contrast to *repá beteáme,* God, Who Lives Above.

The Displacement

In sixty years, according to census figures, the white or mestizo population of the Sierra Tarahumara has doubled. Apart from the land presently occupied by the Rarámuri in the high country and in the deep canyons they used to occupy, according to the annals of the early missionaries who first came to the land of the Rarámuri in 1607, the following were mission centers or places where the Rarámuri lived: the fertile lands of the huge valleys of San Pablo Balleza (which was one of the first Jesuit mission headquarters); San Francisco de Borja (also founded by the Jesuits with the name of the successor of St. Ignatius of Loyola, the founder of the Jesuit order); Papigochi (known today as Ciudad Guerrero); Tomochi, and the immense valley of Matachi. Today, there are no Rarámuri residing in these places. When seen, they are either visiting or seeking work in an orchard or farm.

One hundred years ago Carl Lumholtz, in his stupendous ethnographical study, was impressed at how "The Mexicans" were forcing the Rarámuri from their best lands: "Guachochic...lies in the very midst of the Tarahumare country. It is true that the Mexicans have appropriated all the best land around, and their extensive and fertile ranches lie all around Guachochic. Toward the east, in the direction of the pueblos of Tónachic and Lagunitas, the broad strip of good arable and pasture land as far as Parral is owned exclusively by Mexicans." (Lumholtz, Carl: *Unknown Mexico*, p. 198, Dover Publications, Inc., New York, 1987). "The Indians ascribed the hard times (lack of rain) to the presence of the whites, who had deprived them of their lands as well as of their liberty..." (Ibid., p. 200.) "...When I told him (the richest man in the village) that I liked the Tarahumares, he answered, 'Well, take them with you, every one of them.' All he cared for was their land, and he has already acquired a considerable portion of it." (Ibid., p. 230).

The Rarámuri consider the white man to be an intruder, an invader of the lands that had always been theirs: they feel themselves to be an integral part of the land and of nature, since any indigenous people, of whatever tribe, always believe that the land is a vital, integral part of their lives. And so it is for the Rarámuri, the land being as well the place where God put them: God, which in the Rarámuri concept is Father and Mother at the same time, as is constantly repeated by their "governors" in their sermons or *nawgsaris*.

In contrast, the white man, the non-Rarámuri, is not a son of He Who Lives Above, because he cheats, steals, hoards, invades, and appropriates the land. In addition, he is dishonest in his dealings, and he misuses the forest. Among the worst sins against the moral code of the Rarámuri are lack of brotherhood, impoverishment of another through hoarding, and unwillingness to share. All these things the Rarámuri have experienced at the hand of the whites for centuries, hence the misgivings and the eternal distrust which are felt toward the white man.

Lumholtz notes that "as a rule, the Tarahumare is not a thief in his bargains" (Ibid., pp. 243-244.) "...The Tarahumares are the sons of God, and the Mexicans the sons of the devil..." (Ibid., p. 296). This last is set down by Lumholtz in reference to what the Rarámuri think about the whites and mestizos.

The appropriation of their best lands, which the Rarámuri have suffered across the centuries on a large scale, continues at the present time, slowly but surely. The effects are felt today in the increased hunger, malnutrition and tuberculosis which afflict the Rarámuri, with the result that infant mortality rates are extremely high. According to Lumholtz, the Rarámuri did not always suffer so: "The climate of the sierra, although not so pleasant...is extremely salubrious...Lung diseases are here unknown" (Ibid., p. 207). And he repeats: "Their endurance is truly phenomenal...The wonderful health these people enjoy is really their most attractive trait. They are healthy and look it" (Ibid. p. 241).

At the time during which they possessed all that fertile land in abundance, without doubt no Rarámuri lacked land to plow and plant: they didn't suffer hunger as they do today, nor did they feel the necessity to ask for assistance, or *korima* (which literally means "to share"), as they now have to do in the cities. Unfortunately, this gives the Rarámuri a bad reputation and in certain instances causes social problems.

Brotherhood, Courtesy, And Respect

Respect for another is of primordial importance in the Rarámuri philosophy. For this reason, visitors and tourists should be respectful toward the Rarámuri, as the latter are to others. They give greater value to persons than to objects, to the extent that even business matters are secondary in importance. In their culture, it is a lack of manners to attend to a business matter or to take care of something prior to having taken the time to greet and to attend to people. On arriving where people are gathered, the Rarámuri greet by hand each one of those present, even though there may be many people, given that this greeting is another characteristic mark of their courtesy and of the respect and value they feel for persons over material objects.

On a certain occasion during a chat with a very respected and elderly Rarámuri, a sort of guru to his people, having asked him about the gentile or non-baptized Rarámuri, he simply replied: "I believe that those who love things more than people are more gentile," giving one to understand that, in his judgment, the "chabochi" (as they call the white man and the mestizo), were more pagan than those we call gentiles, just because they are not baptized. In other words, he felt those gentiles to be closer to God because they practiced brotherhood and because, like the baptized Rarámuri – the Pagótuame – they valued people more than material objects, in keeping with their philosophy and culture.

The value they place on persons over objects is practiced with their children as well. These are never chastised, and from the time they are very small they are given the responsibility of making decisions for themselves. They are considered to be adults in the community when they are twelve or thirteen years old. Part of that responsibility is acquired when a child is given, while still quite small, one or two goats. He is their absolute owner, and the parents cannot dispose of them without the consent of the child, the true owner; the offspring of the goats will also belong to the new member of the family. In this manner, and while they are small, they begin acquiring that admirable sense of responsibility which the Rarámuri practice from an early age. Lumholtz mentions the fact: "The young man has his own animals, which he got when he was small, and now his father gives him a piece of land" (Ibid., p. 270).

To be hospitable with their people, or even with strangers who are on a journey or passing through, is also part of their philosophy of great respect toward a person, since practicing brotherhood and sharing their food is, for them, a sacred duty; not to do so is an unpardonable sin. Thus, when one arrives at their houses, he is given a bit of pinole (ground, toasted corn), some beans, tortillas, etc. Among the Tepehuanes there is a saying about the Rarámuri: "...when you go among the Tarahumaras you will never feel hunger." (Robles, R., *El rieno de los Rarámuri pagótuame*, unpublished ms.) And Lumholtz states also: "The first thoughts of a person falling ill are: Whom have I offended? What have I taken that I should have left alone, and what have I kept that I should have given? Then the shaman may tell him to find the person to whom he had refused to give food, and the sick one and his wife go from house to house asking the people: "Was it you whom I refused food?" (Lumholtz, Carl: op cit., p. 315-316).

All this is nothing more than the result of the respect and value they assign to persons, given that even in their poverty they know how to share. Their courtesy is buttressed by that regard felt for people. "...the Tarahumare is a very polite personage. In his language he even has a word 'reko' which is the equivalent of the English 'please', and which he used constantly" (Ibid., p. 258). There do not exist swear words in the Rarámuri vocabulary. They have to use those in Spanish which they have learned from the "chabochi."

Communal Life

Their sense of brotherhood, their obliging nature, their mutual sharing in the lives of one another are all well known: mutual assistance is the norm in agricultural tasks, in the construction of a house or fence, or in any endeavor which requires various persons. As recompense, some pinole or beans and tortillas are shared, but the principal attraction of these endeavors is *teswino* - batari - their typical corn beer. "No man could get his field attended to if he did not at first make ready a good supply of teswino, because beer is the only remuneration his assistants receive." (Ibid., p. 253.)

Mission Activity

The impact of the first missionaries on the religious life of the Rarámuri was great, since they found that the Indians were of good disposition and that the life they led was consistent with the Christian life. The one negative criticism that the ancient missionaries make as one (and in large part I agree with them), was the excessive use of teswino at their feasts and ceremonies, principally because of the consequences of drunkenness on these occasions. This does not mean that in the beginning, the labor of the missionaries was easy. In fact, there was resistance and opposition by individual leaders and by groups. Since the missionaries were outsiders, they were often associated with the invading miners who arrived practically at the same time, and almost always accompanied by soldiers. Obviously, this made the work of the missionaries difficult, and some were martyred in uprisings.

There were flourishing missions at many points in the country inhabited by the Rarámuri. The first was established with the arrival of Father Juan Fonte in 1607, and they lasted until 1767, when by decree of King Charles III of Spain the Jesuits were expelled from their possessions in all of New Spain, which necessarily included the Jesuits who labored in this region.

The expulsion of the Jesuit missionaries meant the abandoning of the missions and leaving the Indians to the tender mercies of the greedy invaders, who little by little forcibly took their best lands until the Indians had disappeared completely from some areas, as noted before. On the other hand, the Franciscan missionaries were unable to fill in for the Jesuits, due to the lack of funds and personnel, and because the wars of independence of the 19th century were hostile to their efforts. (Almada, Francisco R.: *Diccionario de historia, geografía y biografía chihuahuenses*, p. 340, Impresora de Juárez, S.A, Juárez, Chih., Mexico, 1968.) Thus, the missions were effectively abandoned, with but a few diocesan priests attending them, until at the end of the century, the Josephite fathers were in charge, working out of Cusárare.

Christianity In The Rarámuri Mold

Upon being abandoned by the clergy and being left alone for almost a century and a half, the Rarámuri were at liberty to reinterpret what they had learned from the missionaries and to cast their Christianity in their proper symbolical and ritualistic molds, putting aside what was meaningless to them while conserving and adapting the rest according to their cultural and symbolical expression. This would have been impossible for the missionaries to have done, given their conceptual, western frame of mind. For the Rarámuri, what they learned then and what they learn today from their governors, or *siríames,* more than definitions and concepts, is the connection between life and teachings: in other words, they do not know how to verbalize or conceptualize what they have been taught. They must simply do it by giving testimony through their daily lives.

Their Theology

Their theology is not a treatise, nor is it dogma or abstract concepts; hence the difficulty in understanding them by those of us who are used to definitions and precise responses. They have a "Popular Religiosity," or sanctity, very much their own. It is quite rich, surprisingly orthodox in all the basics, and they learn it from life itself, from their relationships with the community, in the *nawésaris* of their *siríames,* and in their ongoing relationship with God. The ancients, or *owirúames* (doctors and spiritual guides), along with the *siríames,* guide and teach the people that Tarahumara theology in the experience of life itself, in their ceremonies, their varied rituals and fiestas, always to the rhythm of daily life and never in impersonal, public dealings, disconnected from life, as ours are wont to be. Therefore, in order to understand them and their theology, the road cannot be to ask them about their theological concepts, since these are never formulated; the only way is to live among them, to observe their lives and their actions, their many fiestas, ceremonies and rituals, which are full of symbolism (Robles, R.: op cit.).

Their truth as children of God lies in their manner of living; their actions are their truth, a truth that necessarily evolves and fits into their daily lives which also change, but always following a rule in harmony with their traditions: these are changes which come about as they live their daily lives, and not because of any theoretical imperatives. This is their religion as practiced in living day to day, and never as a concept (Ibid.).

Rituals And Dance

Upon coming to know the Rarámuri for the first time, one could conclude that their culture and/or their ceremonial rituals are an incomprehensible mish-mash of pagan/Christian signs or symbols. Indeed, this is how they are taken by those who observe them on a superficial level. The majority of the mestizos - the "chabochi," or "bearded ones," as they are called by the Rarámuri - so judge them to be. They do not understand that the ritual, abstracted or reduced to symbols, is what is important in the Rarámuri culture, as opposed to anything of a contemplative nature. Thus, their prayers are symbolized more in the ritual of the dance than in verbal form; and they symbolize the reverent greeting given the cross and the images of the saints by signing across the face and turning the body to the left.

Their symbolism and their ritualistic expressions are often incomprehensible to our conceptual mentality. Because of our western orthodoxy, we find contradictions and inconsistencies in them which disconcert us. But the Rarámuri, who are not given to contemplate over such matters, experience no such conflict. It seems to us a frank inconsistency that they offer food to their dead, but for them this is a duty born of brotherhood: the duty to assist the person who has gone and who is traveling, the person who must gather strength from the aroma of the preferred food which will no longer serve to feed the living, the person who was needed and who was summoned by *onorúame,* He Who Lives Above.

From antiquity, for the Christian Rarámuri, the sun has been the symbol of God, *onorúame,* He Who Is Father-Mother But Is One. The governors always stress in their sermons the monotheistic nature of "Tata-rioshi" (from the Spanish, "Father-God"). They know themselves to be his children, and they feel the duty and obligation to assist him so evil will not triumph over good, as will be seen below. I do not mean to say that they were, nor are today, worshippers of the sun. Quite to the contrary, I mean only that the sun is but the symbol of God. There also exist other myths and legends as regards the moon and the stars, which will not be considered here (cf. Lumholtz, op cit., pp. 297, 324).

Throughout the dance they ask forgiveness, they petition for rain, they give thanks for the rain and the crops; they assist *repá beteáme,* He Who Lives Above, so he will not be defeated by *reré beteáme,* the devil, in order that good can triumph over evil. Apropos the above, Lumholtz writes that "...afterward the rain seemed almost to pursue me, much to the delight of the Indians I visited, who had been praying and dancing for rain for a long time" (Ibid., p. 201). "Dancing not only expresses prayers for rain and life, but also petitions God to ward off evil in any shape, as diseases of man, beast or crops" (Ibid., p. 332).

Ancestrally, the Rarámuri possessed the ritual dance of *yúmari or tutuguri.* In this dance, food offerings are made to God; at the climatic moment, *wiroma,* the offerings, are directed to the four cardinal points, and God is nourished by the aroma of the offerings, which he then blesses. Probably the ritual of today is the same as the ancestral form. However, since they know and feel themselves to be children of the one and true God, the Father-Mother, they have Christianized the ritual and they perform it in the spirit of being children of God, and so they cement the community bonds which unite them in the brotherhood of being children of the same Father-Mother.

Another dance, that of the *matachines,* is not autochthonous, but was introduced by the missionaries. It was accepted by the Rarámuri and integrated into their ritual ceremonies to such a degree that it can be considered a native dance in their culture and fiestas, principally those of the Catholic calendar: Our Lady of Guadalupe, Christmas, the Epiphany, Corpus Christi, Candlemas Day (the feast of the purification of the Virgin) and other saints' days. The dance of the matachines is also included in many of their rituals and fiestas that are truly indigenous in nature. Generally, when Yúmari is danced, apart from the cross or crosses used (which are not of Christian origin) and the place of the offerings, another cross is provided for the matachines. This seems to be an attempt, given their symbolic cast of mind, to Christianize the ritual.

The dance of the matachines appears to have originated at Comelico Superiore in the province of Venice to the north of Italy, almost bordering the Austrian Tyrol. There, even today, this dance is performed at carnival. The costumes are basically the same, although here they are of more modest materials. The name of the dance is the same: *Matazin.* They use some wooden masks, as are used here by the *chapeyones,* those who lead the dance (cf. Ianniello,

Cristina, "Il Carnavale a Comelico Superiore," *Mondo Ladino XII,* pp. 1-4, 1988).

Holy Week

At present the principal celebration of the Rarámuri Pagótuame are the feasts of Holy Week, *noríroacbi* – when they go round and round – during which they will place arches of pine boughs to mark the place of the multiple turns taken by the processions of these festivities. Originally these were taught to them by the missionaries, who tried to stage gospel passages from Holy Week. These stage representations were so pleasing to the Indians that multitudes were attracted, as the ancient missionaries relate with great pleasure, and they enjoyed tremendous acceptance by the Indians of the entire region. These are celebrated wherever there is a church and they basically follow the same pattern, albeit with certain regional differences and adaptations, as can be proven today, even though they have not had the presence of a priest for years. In reality they begin on Candlemas day – February 2 – with the sounding of the drum, which they play exclusively during Lent, and with the naming of the "Pharisees" in great numbers in which many people participate.

Two principal groups take part in these fiestas of Holy Week: the Pharisees and the soldiers, both of which have their captains to lead them. The Pharisees carry white flags, and the soldiers red. (In certain villages, there are other groups, such as *the pintos* in Norogachi, the *mulatos,* with their blackened faces, in Tónachi, and the Moors in Samachiki). Also participating are the *tenancbes,* who are in charge of bearing the images of the saints and the incense during the procession. On the last day of the fiesta, the *pascoleros* dance the merry pascol to the sound of violins and flutes, wearing jingling bells around their ankles.

But for us, the non-Indians, the Holy Week ceremonies of the Rarámuri are the most difficult to understand. though they were accepted from the beginning with great joy and pleasure, upon having been left alone at the departure of the Jesuits, the Rarámuri continued to celebrate these fiestas which they had taken for their own; however, from the religious point of view, little by little they forgot the allegory and imbued them with symbolism from their own history, much as the Spaniards had done with their representations of the struggle between Moors and Christians. In an admirably uniform manner throughout the region, the Rarámuri symbolized the "chabochis" through the "Pharisees," the evil ones, who are painted white to represent the chabochis. These are the partisans of Judas, and in the dance they are symbolized as being everywhere and in control of the situation, until they are finally defeated by the soldiers, who represent the ultimate triumph of good.

The judas is an important figure in these festivities. He is usually a straw man, always dressed as a chabochi with oversized genitals, who is jeered by all until he is put to death, being burned, or shot, or pierced through by arrows. In Creel, as in other places, burlesque placards are hung on the Judas. On these are pictured the outrages the Rarámuri have suffered from those who exploit and oppress them. In this manner, they give vent to their rage through the judas. Robles well states the point: "Holy Week is impressive because it manifests the repudiation of the chabochi scheme in a ritual, yet brutal manner" (Robles, R., op cit.).

The pascoleros of Samachiki symbolize the Resurrection in a most significant manner. After having danced for several hours during the morning of Holy Saturday, when the bells ring out for glory at about noon and during the high point of the dance, one of the dancers releases a little bird inside the church. This *chuyépari*, or "wall hopper," had previously been carried in a little basket at the dancer's waist. The death of the Pharisees is next in the order of events. These personages roll about on the floor of the church, striking their wooden swords on the floor, until they leave the church howling in terror; they then run around the church, knocking down the arches on the way of the cross and tearing the ornamental feathers from their heads. The judas is put to death, and the battle between the Pharisees and soldiers takes place.

Offices And Religious Rites

The ancient missionaries attempted to assemble the Indians together by having them live in villages so as to simplify communications, but they only succeeded in convincing them to hold their meetings at the church, which the Indians called the village. Having thus organized them, the missionaries also exercised great influence as regards the offices and religious rites which exist down to the present in Rarámuri communities. The principal office is that of the Governor, the *siríame*, or headman and spiritual guide of the community; he also judges disputes, which are settled in a tranquil manner more through counseling than by the imposition of sanctions, so that peace and harmony can be restored to the community. The *siríames* are elected by common accord, and the Rarámuri always choose the most upright and prestigious individual in the community. These do not lead by following a personal standard, but rather by following a communal consensus.

We do not know whether the missionary Jesuits, when they left, delegated the performance of certain religious rites, such as performing baptisms, the rites of matrimony, directing meetings at the church, etc. There is very little documentation in this respect, given that the contemporary archives were sent to the Franciscan Convent at Guadalupe, Zacatecas, never to reach their destination. There exist only letters which had been sent to the provincial house of the Jesuits in Mexico and to the house general in Rome (these are now to be found in the National Archives of Mexico and in the Archives of Parral). The fact is that the Rarámuri assumed, either through their own volition or by having been delegated to do so, the role of performing certain rites that the missionary fathers normally exercised: marrying the betrothed, performing rites of baptism perhaps equivalent to the baptism formerly received from the missionaries (or a similar rite already existed among them, and this is why the rite of baptism blended so harmoniously into their culture), meeting to pray in church, and above all, the instruction and spiritual guidance given the community by the *siríames,* or governors. It is through their assiduous *nawésaris,* or sermons, that they teach, counsel, and guide the community; through these sermons, their teachings, their theology and moral code, and their traditions are transmitted.

In order that he can comply with his duties, the *siríame* counts on the assistance of multiple subordinates: generals, captains, mayors, constables, foremen, *chapeyones, abanderados, tenanches,* and *resanderos* (the last four are personages of the fiesta). These posts (which vary from one village to another) are conferred by the *siríame,* but always with the concurrence of the people and of the chosen person. These are positions of public service and are not positions of power or lucre. Although no economic benefit inures to the officeholders, they do enjoy a certain prestige. The position is not held for any determinate period of time, but only for so long as the community is satisfied with the manner in which its duties are discharged (Ibid).

Among the Rarámuri, the priest is also considered as someone who holds a position designated by them. His role is to counsel with or advise any of them, including the *siríame.* The priest is the one who baptizes and who marries them on occasion, given that they have their proper rites and ministers, who directs the church ceremonies, who celebrates Mass, and who is the expert in the matters of God and who speaks to them of him.

The office that the healer, or *owirúame,* exercises among them is somewhat similar. He is the principal personage in the ceremonies of life, illness or death, and he plays an important role in the lives of all Rarámuri. Each Rarámuri has his own *owirúame,* under whose keeping he is placed at a very young age. "These priest-doctors have their specialties. Some sing only at *rutubury or yúmari* dances, others only at híkuli feasts...They all conscientiously fast and pray, complying with the demands of the gods(?), which impose restrictions and abstinence, and they are therefore called I 'righteous men' *(owirúamí).* They are the wise men of the tribe; and as rainmakers, healers, and keepers of the heritage of tribal wisdom and traditions, their influence is powerful" (Lumholtz, Carl: op cit., p. 312).

A Different Culture Is Not Inferior

This brief sketch of some life experiences, along with an outline of some aspects of the Rarámuri culture, teach us that their culture is totally different but not inferior to ours. It is simply different, with human relations that are a thing of beauty, as Collier notes (Collier, John: op cit., pp. 17-20), and full of lessons for us. Lumholtz expands: "Luckily, withal, the Tarahumare has not yet been wiped out of existence...it may take a century yet before they will all be made the servants of the whites and disappear...Future generations will not find any other record of the Tarahuamares than what scientists of the present age can elicit from the lips of the people and from the study of their implements and customs. They stand out today as an interesting relic of a time long gone by; as a representative of one of the most important stages in the development of the human race; as one of those wonderful primitive tribes that were the founders and makers of the history of mankind." (Lumholtz, Carl: op cit., pp. 420421.)

I believe it to be opportune, in concluding this brief essay, to quote the words of Luigi Fabbris, a young Italian who worked here at the mission among the Rarámuri, and who has recently written me: "...the Rarámuri have much to teach, they know how to struggle for life and for survival, I hope that they never feel embarrassment because they are Indians, but instead feel secure in their surroundings. But if their lands are taken from them and their corn is consumed, if they are made to be psychodependents without autonomy, without liberty and without their proper conscience, they will not be able to succeed in their cultural model. Humanity will be poorer without the Tarahumaras. The Tarahumara model is humanity itself, it is the voice of the ages and the millennia. They are not savages, they are a message in poetry for us the true savages and despoilers. To make them become extinct, or to make them disappear is suicide for us. Without them, not a few prophets of peace, tranquility, frugality, and of the symbiotic relationship with nature will disappear. They are a message of salvation for our supposedly civilized existence, Because of this, I must return in the future, that I may hear the voice of these John the Baptists, the Rarámuri."

CLINICA STA TERESITA

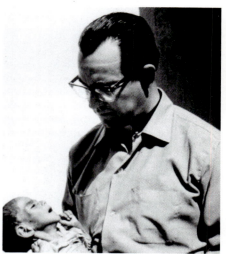

Luis G. Verplancken, S.J.

*Luis G. Verplancken, S.J. has
provided aid to the Tarahumara in the most critical
times. Currently the
Tarahumara face the biggest
change in their history due to
deforestation, famine, and
cholera. He is there for them
now and will be in
the future.*

TARAHUMARA CHILDREN'S HOSPITAL IN CREEL
PRESERVING A HERITAGE, ENSURING A FUTURE, A NEW SOCIAL COMPLEX

Health Care

In order to attend to the human to right health care of the
Raramuri, the Tarahumara Mission found it necessary to
establish three hospitals in the region. The hospital in
Creel, the Clínica Santa Teresita, was established in 1965.
Today the hospital has 75 beds for children and adults, 6
doctors, 35 nurses, and the most indispensable services of
any hospital: pharmacy, laboratory, operating rooms, X-
rays, maternity ward, dental clinic, etc. More than 7,000
Tarahumara (mostly children) are cared for at the hospital
yearly. The services furnished them are free. In order to
continue offering this service, the only full-service hospital
available to the Tarahumara, it is vital that revenue come
from other sources. A tax-deductible non-profit corpora-
tion in the United States was established so that U.S. donors
could have their donations to the hospital legally deduct-
ible. The U.S. agency is Tarahumara Children's Hospital
Fund, 330 Crystal Street, New Orleans, LA 70124.

Education

If the Tarahumara need anything from the outside, it is
education. To help accomplish this goal, the clinic built
two rural boarding schools in the area, one near Creel and
the other in rural Rejogochi. Some 90 young Indians are
there 5 days a week boarding and learning. At school they
are taught hygiene, poultry farming, husbandry, craft making, basic math, and Spanish. The school provides food,
clothing, shelter, and instructors.

Food Distribution

Even in the best of times, the Tarahumara Indians living
in the steep wooded mountains, barely produce enough
corn and beans to keep alive. Under the direction of the
Clínica Santa Teresita the project of purchasing and distrib-
uting food continues to be the saving component for these
destitute people. Some community work is required when
provisions are delivered so that the recipients can maintain
their dignity. Around 240 deliveries are made yearly to 140
different Indian communities. An average of 400 tons of
staple food are distributed yearly by the clinic.

Well Drilling

Clean drinking water is basic to life. A great percentage of
the Tarahumara children's health problems can be attrib-
uted to polluted water causing digestive illness, typhoid,
parasites, and severe infections. A freshwater well project
was begun by the clinic in 1995. And in the communities
where the shallow wells have been dug, they now bring
decent drinking water to the Indians for the first time. "Ever
since we have clean water from wells, our children do not
get sick like they used to" says a Tarahumara father.

The Majestic Barrancas
by Richard D. Fisher

It is said that there are five canyons in the state of Chihuahua which are deeper and larger than the Grand Canyon of the Colorado. The first descent and exploration of the two deepest and narrowest of these canyons was accomplished in 1986. It is amazing that these incredible chasms have not been documented in the modern era. It took the development of canyoneering techniques to make these areas accessible to exploration and documentation.

For years, the great barrancas of Mexico have been recognized as some of the wildest, most rugged and interesting areas on the North American continent. Parts of the barrancas country have been explored since the days of Carl Lumholtz (1890). In 1892, Lumholtz accomplished on foot what is to date the most complete exploration of the Sierra Madre and the Barranca de Sinforosa. Carl Lumholtz called this canyon the Barranca de San Carlos, and his work still stands today as the most accurate and complete account of the area. As far as I know, no effort has been made to explore all the canyons in the region by raft or other watercraft. In 1985 I set out to accomplish this goal.

The objectives of this four-year project was to document and evaluate the barrancas for National Park status, accomplish a preliminary survey of flora, fauna, and human uses, and to compare these gorges to similar systems worldwide in terms of river-running potential. An effort was also made to draw comparisons between these little-known canyonlands to its more famous sister system—the Grand Canyon of the Colorado.

In January of 1986 I organized a team of expert expeditioners to explore the Barranca de Sinforosa, the second deepest and the narrowest chasm in the area. We experienced many incredible difficulties due to the extreme low water. We were, however, successful in locating an area which is largely undisturbed by the activities of man. This is one of the only areas in the entire region to maintain flora and fauna that were common throughout the canyons when the missionaries arrived with goats and cattle 300 years ago. In October 1986, a second successful first descent was made of the deepest Barranca, the Urique.

General Description – Río Verde And The Barranca De Sinforosa

The Río Verde is the largest of the three rivers which drain the central "Sierra de Tarahumara." This river maintains the highest output of water annually. The Río Verde is, practically speaking, the most remote and difficult to reach of the three river systems. The three sister rivers are Río Urique, Río Batopilas, and Río Verde.

It is generally believed that these three rivers carve the largest and deepest canyons in North America, and that these barrancas are certainly one of the greatest canyon systems on earth.

Due to the remote and inaccessible nature of the Río Verde, it is one of the least explored and documented areas in North America.

The flora and fauna of the canyon have been greatly affected and changed by human use, primarily through grazing of cattle and goats. There is a spectacular exception to this in the narrowest area, where a pristine forest with exotic trees, birds, and mammals make their last stand against human encroachment.

The geology of the canyon is primarily hard igneous strata. This exceptionally hard stone is tremendously resistant to erosion. This causes the river channel to be filled with boulders of dramatic proportions. The gradient of the river is also extreme. The estimated drop through the narrows averages 120 feet per mile.

The canyon is used extensively by both Mexicans and Indian families. Tarahumara and Tepehuan Indians are not as abundant as anticipated, and generally inhabit the upper third of the canyon. However, we noted at least one Tarahumara family living in a temporary camp at river level.

The Río Verde is not navigable at any water level with the equipment or techniques available today. Short sections of the canyon can be backpacked, as there is trail access in numerous areas. Downriver travel is not practical except for short distances (1-2 miles). Expedition member Tim Bathen suggested that Buck Rogers-type jet packs might one day make this barranca accessible.

Due to the extreme depth, narrowness, and geology of the Barranca de Sinforosa, the basic principles of rapids formation are not the same as in the Colorado river system. Almost all rapids on the Colorado river system are created by boulders washed into the river channel from side canyons. While some of the largest boulder fields in the Sinforosa Canyon are created in this way, the vast majority of boulder fields and rapids (waterfalls) are created by slabs that fall directly into the river's course from above.

The canyon is not as consistent as the Grand Canyon of the Colorado in terms of narrowness x depth x length. Overall, I estimate that the Sinforosa canyon is slightly larger than the Grand Canyon. The Sinforosa does not appear larger because, as well as being very narrow, it twists and turns so that views over fifty miles in length are uncommon.

As previously noted, this canyon is not suitable for any type of traditional river travel. However, by using "canyoneering" techniques, it is possible (although not practical) to traverse 30-40 miles on a well-planned and well conceived expedition. The average mileage per day, under the best of conditions, should be planned at 3-5 miles.

The weather during the first expedition and exploration, which occurred during January, was characteristic as cool-to cold nights and warm-to-hot days. Previous to our expedition, there had been little significant rainfall or snow for three months. The river was at a lower water level than expected, presenting major problems. Some of the rapids would have been runnable at higher water, but that would have made conditions even more perilous in the boulder fields.

The members of the expedition team were: Tim Bathen, Michael Kelly, and team leader Richard Fisher.

General Description – Barranca de Urique

Carl Lumholtz reports the word 'Urique' means canyon in Tarahumara. There is often confusion concerning the actual locations to which this name is applied.

Generally speaking, the village of Urique is located in the upper portion of Barranca de Urique. This canyon terminates at the Río Fuerte. It is not common knowledge that downstream of the Fuerte-Urique junction is a smaller but incredibly beautiful canyon which I shall call the Fuerte Canyon.

The Urique and Fuerte Canyons are the only areas in the barrancas which lend themselves to any type of traditional river travel. I emphasize that they are only runnable during high but not flood-stage water.

Below the town of Urique the river can be run for approximately ten miles before it is necessary to portage about one-half mile. This place, Dos Arroyas, is where a thick patch of large boulders create several small but beautiful waterfalls. This is one of the most spectacular areas of the trip. Depending on the water level, it is possible to run almost every rapid from here to the Río Fuerte. It takes approximately three days to run from Urique Village to the Fuerte River.

This entire run can be described as passing through drug cultivation country. I advise that rafters stay on the river and not do any side hiking at all. Usually Mexican people are very friendly and safe to deal with, but in this area avoidance is recommended. Let the local people come to you; don't seek them out, as you might run into something unexpected and unpleasant if you go exploring.

At the village of Tubares, there is the beautiful ruin of an early mission. Be careful in this village not to explore beyond the mission area. Downstream from Tubares is another mission called El Realito, which to this day is still standing. It's a beautiful and enchanting spot. Approximately five miles downstream of El Realito, several rapids are encountered which end in a very dangerous waterfalls/shoot. We were able to line the raft through this area.

Five miles below the falls, the San Francisco Dam is encountered. The river has breached the dam so there is no lake. However, the dam itself is a mandatory portage. Below the dam is the heart of the Río Fuerte Canyon. There are a few small ripples here. The water generally has a good current in this area, but appears to be very still. Crocodiles once lived in this part of the canyon. The San Francisco Dam site is incorrectly marked on the topographical maps. It is one-and-one-half days from the dam to the takeout at the Agua Caliente train station.

Overall, the trip can be made in about six days *on the river* with appropriate water level, equipment, and techniques.

What we found at the end of the expedition is very discouraging. Right before the takeout at the famous "Copper Canyon Train," a large dam is under construction. It's truly a shame that the deepest canyon in the hemisphere will be drowned before it is fully documented scientifically or enjoyed by outdoor enthusiasts.

Expedition members were: Kerry Kruger, Rick Brunton and the team leader, Richard Fisher.

General Description – Barranca del Cobre (Copper Canyon)

Previous expeditions to the Barranca del Cobre produced some very valuable information. Due to the relative ease of access via the famous Copper Canyon Railroad and through Creel, the Barranca del Cobre has been the site of many professional and amateur expeditions. Several attempts have been made to descend the river. The general consensus is that the Barranca del Cobre is unsuitable for any type of traditional river travel. Most, if not all expeditions to this canyon, have not been able to achieve their objectives due to the extreme nature of the riverbed terrain, inappropriate techniques, and equipment not suitably adapted to canyon topography.

The Barranca del Cobre is made impassable by a huge boulder pile and waterfalls which occur approximately ten miles downstream of the Umira bridge. This boulder field is where the river goes underground for over a mile. Downstream, the river course assumes a nature much like the Sinforosa Canyon (see photographs). Several other areas have also been tried by boat and or kayak. One is from El Tejaban to the trail down from El Divisadero. This stretch is also described as unrunnable. One party seemed to have a little better luck in inflatable kayaks from the El Divisadero trail put-in to the village of Urique.

The Barranca De Guaynopa

It is interesting to note that the Río Aros is, as a practical matter, the largest river in northwest Mexico. Now that the Yaqui River no longer exists due to hydroelectric projects, the Aros stands out as the most significant wild river in this region. The Río Aros, which is called the Río Sirupa as it cuts the Guaynopa Canyon in what is called the "big bend," shares many characteristics with the Barranca del Cobre. This area is near Madera–Chihuahua.

National Park Status

There is no national park or natural preserve established anywhere in the barrancas area. The canyons dissecting this region of the Sierra Madre are world renowned for their scenic grandeur and spectacular vistas. It might be considered that several "units" in the barrancas country would be a feasible concept for establishing national parks preserves.

The narrowest section of the Barranca de Sinforosa would make an excellent candidate for national park designation and preservation. There would be few conflicts with other interests in the "narrows," as this particular area has maintained the natural integration of flora, fauna, and scenic wonders.

The specific area which would fit all the criteria for national park status is where the San Rafael Ranch is now located on the rim of the canyon.

The Barranca de Batopilas is discussed more thoroughly in the Lost Cathedral section of this guidebook. The area surrounding Satevo would make an ideal location for a national historical zone or park.

In the Barranca del Cobre, the best location for a national park would be from the Umira Bridge to the El Divisadero area, as this is the most spectacular section of the canyon.

In the United States, these areas would be considered too small and incomplete for national park status. Considering the political, economic, and social situation in Mexico, these areas would make an excellent start and are certainly the gemstone areas of the Majestic Barrancas of the Sierra Madre.

Geographical Information

Name	Depth in Meters	Feet	Location
Urique Canyon	1879	6136	10 km. S. of Urique
Sinforosa Canyon	1830	6002	C. de Guerachi
Batopilas Canyon	1800	5904	10 km. N. of Batopilas
Copper Canyon (Barranca del Cobre)	1760	5770	At Urique
Guaynopa Canyon	1620	5313	15 km. N. El Paraja Bridge
Grand Canyon	1425	4674	Hopi Point

The Lost Cathedral
by Richard D. Fisher

Isolated deep in the most remote and rugged barrancas country is a great anomaly in space and time. Its name unknown, its creator unidentified, its very existence questioned. Local myths contradict each other as to its origins and purpose.

Many of the missions and colonial churches in northwestern Mexico are well documented and frequently visited. There are, however, persistent rumors that a great cathedral exists deep in the Grand Canyon in Mexico. Unaccounted for, shrouded in mystery and legend. Having accidently discovered many unknown places in the northern Sierras, my interest in exploring these areas was aroused. I set out to scout the central Sierra Tarahumara and to find this "Lost Cathedral" and its picturesque canyon setting.

I first heard of the grand church, hidden deep in the barrancas country, from an ancient adventurer. Fifteen years ago I was considering a backpacking expedition to the famous "Grand Canyon of Mexico" near the town of Creel, Chihuahua. As I spoke to many people with knowledge of the area concerning this trip, the best information came from a gentleman who retired from years of exploration, settling down to manage a travel agency in Tucson. Although, as the years pass I can't remember his name, I'll never forget the astounding story he told me.

In a cool, dusty office surrounded by colorful travel posters and brochures, he related the following tale: Down the river from the small village of Batopilas is a fantastic cathedral, the most interesting man-made object in the entire canyon country. He described the canyon setting as one of the most beautiful scenes he had encountered during his world-wide travels. His description was painted with such vivid color that, in my mind's eye, I could visualize a great romantic painting depicting the ruins of an ancient monolith, draped with vines, and canyon walls rising to the very heavens.

He told of a group of visitors that wanted to take the cathedral's bells to display in a museum. Respectfully, the Indians told them they could take the bells, but they could not leave the valley. The collectors decided that their lives were more important than the church bells, and departed peacefully.

During my early research, I talked with several people who had been to Batopilas and heard that a few Tucsonans had even been to the mission. However, even with careful research, I could find no map which indicated its location, no photographs, and no one who could tell me who built it, when it was constructed, or why. Everyone who had visited the barrancas country was in agreement on one thing: that the country was incredibly rugged and travel to the Batopilas area was, at best, very difficult. Conflicting reports concerning road conditions and general travel hazards led me to prepare for the worst. I was outfitted with the minimum: a backpack, camping gear, food, water and, only basic photographic equipment.

I traveled with another explorer who had extensive outdoor experience. We both harbored a keen interest in the Barrancas of Mexico – which had been at our doorstep for years.

The train ride to Copper Canyon was all that it is written up to be. We shared a modern coach with a few other tourists. A bilingual interpreter gave us a detailed description of the various panoramas encountered along the track. When she in English, her tones were very soft and each word was enunciated with gentle precision. Several times I asked her repeat the description. Carefully, she would repeat each on with accuracy and cheerfully answer my questions.

When asked questions concerning the geology or the geography of the area, she had surprisingly good answers, but would indicate she was not 100% sure they were correct. I felt like I was on a first class airline, and not a rough train ride winding through rugged deserts, canyons, and mountains.

The views were spectacular! At the Témoris station, I hopped off to photograph a three-jump waterfall cascading from a narrow cleft. The train stopped to take on another engine for the steepest part of the climb. Looking up the track, I could see an "S" turn on a very precipitous incline.

I rushed into position for a shot about twenty feet down the hill. The whistle sounded as I reached the best vantage point. I figured with the steep climb, the train would get off to a slow start. Firing off the first shot, I heard the train leap forward.

The clash of car linkages meant business. Before the second shot, I looked up to see the train running full speed up the mountain. People were yelling for me to run. I felt confident I could outrun a train grinding uphill from a dead stop. About three strides up the rocky slope I realized the train could set world records. Zero to sixty in seconds, or so it seemed. I was sprinting alongside, visualizing hobo stories I heard as a kid about people being sliced up by trains. As an open portal swished past, I lifted my camera so the passengers could grab it, and I could swing myself onto the hand rail. They grabbed my entire arm and swung me physically onto the landing. "Muchas Gracias" was said all around, amid smiles and laughter. Another average day on the Barranca del Cobre Vista Dome rail tour. I usually take at least three shots (photos) for safety; in this case one would have to do.

The train climbed through the canyons from desert scrub to alpine forest in two hours. Another five-minute stop at the famous "Grand Canyon of Mexico Overlook" and a second sprint back to the impatient train. I was a bit conservative after the first whistle and stepped aboard just as the train lurched forward. The Divisadero stop was incredible. The whole panoramic view of the Barranca del Cobre was spread out below, as Tarahumara children sold simple baskets and carved dolls along the guard rails.

Arriving in Creel late in the afternoon, crisp alpine air greeted the passengers at the station. A mountain town with a sawmill, several churches, a tourist shop, and a few hotels, Creel could be "anywhere Old-West U.S.A." Sort of a nondescript village with pot-holed streets and hardy, honest mountain folk. Mule trains and horses were as frequent as pickup trucks.

We quickly learned that a bus actually ran to Batopilas at least once a week and sometimes twice. We could also catch "regular" buses to other remote areas. Mountain buses are the only "rapid transit" available to local families. They serve anyone and *everyone* who needs a ride. This makes for jampacked terrestrial ships wallowing through a jumbled sea of dusty canyons. Instead of waiting the couple of days for the bus, we caught a ride on a lumber truck leaving the sawmill the next morning. Headed back into the mountains, these huge flat beds fan out over a thousand square miles to pick up freshly cut timber.

The first or second truck stopped and we exchanged greetings. I asked the driver where he was headed, but could not understand his reply. Fortunately, I did understand we were headed in the same direction and jumped aboard.

Bumping along the road, a Tarahumara woman and two small children shared the back of the open flat-bed truck with us. We crowded together so that no one would be thrown off into the ditch – or worse.

Every half hour or so, the truck halted for a short break. At each stop, I would show the driver the map and ask where he was headed. Even though he wasn't able to point it out, he did assure us that it was near Batopilas. Guachochi (an Indian name) kept turning around and around in my mind. Finally I realized it was a "major" town – all the way across the canyon country, near the Barranca de Sinforosa. We were in luck! On the first day out, we hitched a ride across the Sierra to a town near our mystery canyon.

I had two objectives for the expedition: to find the lost cathedral, and to visit the largest and most spectacular canyon in Mexico.

All day long, we lurched down one mountain and bounded up another. The Tarahumara mother got off well before noon and disappeared down a steep ravine with her small children trotting along behind. Various people enjoyed our driver's generosity during the day, as the truck continued to stop for mountain folk standing beside the road. It was actually less than one hundred miles, but it took six hours to traverse the canyon-cut mountains. We met more than a dozen people during our ride.

Upon reaching our destination of Guachochi, I discovered a new found respect for rodeo bull riders. I felt as though I had had a spinal fusion operation from my tail bone all the way to my jaw. My hand was frozen on the logging chain stretched around the bed of the truck, after grasping for safety for so long. My teeth were clenched so tight (so as not to lose any) that it was hard to open my mouth to say "Muchas Gracias!" The driver took his "tip" to the local cantina and we limped off looking for a hotel.

The next morning, we woke well before dawn and stuffed a few scraps of wood in the stove to heat coffee and thaw our boots. Our hotel was a modern two-story stone structure with a small wood stove in each room. I was a little nervous pouring kerosene over pine chips in the predawn darkness. The smell of raw petroleum leaping into flame brought back faint memories of my grandmother starting the breakfast fire on our Indiana farm, as my child's appetite demanded oatmeal with honey.

This morning started with hot coffee and cold tortillas. Outside our hotel, there was anticipation in the air as our frosty breath was tinted gold by the rising sun. We hired a pickup truck to take us to the edge of Mexico's greatest canyon.

On the rim, the excitement intensified as a warming sun began to drive lacy clouds out of the canyon, to drift over distant pine-clad mesas. We couldn't wait to explore this mysterious chasm, so down we plunged.

Canyons are amazingly deceptive. We actually leapt down vertically two or three feet with each step, yet hours later we were still high along the canyon wall. If it were a mountain of the same vertical proportions, we would have realized it would take at least one day to descend and would have planned two or more days for the ascent.

Through the blistering heat of day, we plunged downward. Passing from pines to oaks, we finally entered the desert life zone. I was limping badly when we reached the river. It had been the longest, steepest trail I had encountered in fifteen years of wilderness travel. The Barranca de Sinforosa is deeper than the Grand Canyon of the Colorado, with this major trail being as rough as the Boucher Trail.

This backpacking expedition was critical to my future appreciation and understanding of the lost mission. While nursing an injured knee for the next two days, I had time to reflect on the mystery surrounding this colossal structure. My throbbing knee prevented me from joining my tougher partner on daily excursions, but it brought home the reality of this country. Often described as some of the most rugged terrain in the world, the barrancas resisted the intrusions of western development for over 300 years. Exceptions to this rule are the mission at Satevó, founded before 1750, and the nearby mining town of Batopilas, built between 1880 and 1910. How the early Fathers constructed one of the largest buildings in the North American West (pre-1920), at the bottom of one of the world's deepest canyons, was a question that intrigued me. Who and when were of interest, but why? *WHY* was the biggest question in my mind.

Imagine one man working alone in a foreign country, with wild tribesmen speaking an isolated dialect in an aggressively hostile environment. One human, with a dream no one else could see, building a great structure using the voluntary labor of aborigines who had never seen an adobe hut; a people who lived in caves and brush shelters. Picture something greater than a building; envision a symbol of faith - anticipate the physical expression of the universal spirit. (Today, national parks are an expression of the same ideal.)

Resting along one of the world's least known rivers, deep in the heart of one of the earth's greatest canyons, these thoughts made me realize how humble many modern outdoor stunts of this era really are. It also impressed upon me the reality that faith can be used for important tasks *other* than moving mountains. Mountains and canyons are God's most inspiring handwork. Great churches are the physical expression of faith and another beautiful creation, the human spirit.

Four days later and just fifty miles away as the raven flies, we were in Batopilas. We hired a mule to carry our packs out of the Barranca de Sinforosa and hitchhiked around to this isolated yet prosperous village. Historically one of the richest towns in Mexico, Batopilas was built by the silver that was mined there. Still one of Mexico's major exports, the silver magnet has drawn men from four continents to this remote locale. With them they brought the skills to build a beautiful town and turn large amounts of metal from the earth.

The Batopilas ore was first discovered in the late sixteenth century. Mines were developed and passed from company to company through the years. The town's fortunes rose and fell with the production of silver and current political conditions. Most of the beautiful buildings in Batopilas today were built between 1880 and 1910, when the area enjoyed a consistent political climate and a high rate of silver production.

While Mexican silver paid for the beautiful town, an American pragmatist named Alexander R. Shepherd was the driving power behind the mine's most productive years. Shepherd spent much of his life building up the Batopilas area. He always reinvested the profits from operations back into more efficient machinery and community improvements such as bridges, aqueducts, and electrification. It wasn't until a few years after his death that investors began to receive regular dividends.

Most of Shepherd's achievements are now in ruins. The Hacienda de San Miguel, which served as the family residence, business office, mill, and reduction plant, is located across the river from Batopilas. Exploring these ruins, one can feel the grandeur of days past, and admire the vision which was responsible for construction of a beautiful place.

While the material wealth of Batopilas vanished with the closing of the mines, its cultural traditions are still rich. Shepherd's son, Grant, describes how the first piano was shipped to Batopilas. The upright piano was carried 185 miles across mountains and deep canyons. Twenty-four carriers working in three shifts would spell each other every 20-30 minutes. It took 15-20 days to make the trip. Most of the carriers were said to be Tarahumaras, who were paid $1.00 a day for their efforts.

The era of prodigious production ended with the revolution, but the mines were still being worked into the mid-1940s. The result of this historical drama, with its many interesting antecedents, is a modern Shangri-la set deep in a remote canyon beside an emerald green river.

Four miles down the river is the great church, whose past, like its future, drifts directionlessly, anchored only by the physical durability of its red brick construction.

Like a mirage set in an unlikely environment, this "cathedral" stands gracefully out of place. Canyon walls and the river are its only appropriate companions. Technically, a cathedral is the seat of a bishop. However, the size and structural complexity of this mission necessitates more than the usual definition of "church." If mountains and canyons are cathedrals fashioned by God, then Satevo must be a cathedral built by faith – for the spirit.

Besides, if it were a church, for whom was it built? There is no record of any sizeable population living near Satevo. Batopilas is the only real village within a five day's horseback ride. Early accounts from Batopilas indicate it took most of a day to ride to Satevo and return. Historically, Batopilas has always had a church large enough to meet its spiritual needs. There are no ruins, roads, large mines, or other signs of previous habitation. Today, there are a dozen or so families living in the Satevo valley. However, these scattered adobe homes wouldn't really qualify as a small village.

Oral tradition, like written documentation, is at best sketchy and varies from source to source. There is agreement on two points – it is very old and very beautiful.

Personally, upon close inspection, I would not say that the structure itself is "beautiful." The mission shows the ravages of time, and stabilization efforts were geared to its preservation, not restoration. Yet, Satevo stands tall and handsome, bearing the weight of time with graceful dignity.

Beauty is a value which is perceived differently from person to person, just as values themselves vary. I once read that if you carry beauty with you in your heart, that values will be your guide.

When I finally reached my physical destination, I had no idea what to expect, and in a way, I really didn't expect anything. The mild February sunlight warmed aching muscles and bones, and shone with tranquil softness on the cathedral. It was easy to just sit, rest, and contemplate the scene. An old Indian drifted up and sat nearby. I asked him who built the mission, when, and why? He told me it was built for the Indians who worked the many silver and gold mines in the surrounding hills. He related that it was very old-the oldest grand cathedral in all of northern Mexico. He said it was so old that no one knew who had constructed it.

He asked me if I wanted a tour of the "missions." Passing through the portal, my self-appointed guide assured me that I was inspecting the original carved oak doors which had been carried down from the "high" mountains by mules. They were more like huge gates than doors, and pushing through them I could understand why the primitive Indians felt they were passing from the natural world into the very presence of God. A stone ceiling arched a full three stories above the great empty chamber. Flagstones, worn smooth by the passing of hundreds of years and thousands of bare feet, covered the resting places of several padres, my guide related reverently in hushed tones.

The old Indian told me many things, but much was lost in translation and to the sunbeams filtering in through cracks and windows high above. I did hear him say that the local people were trying hard to repair the cathedral before it was split asunder by the huge crack that ran the full length of the ancient structure. I could see that work was being done in the vaults high overhead. I gave him a few thousand pesos. He was very thankful and stowed the bills, along with many others, in the holy shrine at the altar.

Outside, I took a few photographs, picked up my backpack, and began to hike back up the canyon. At the last turn in the trail, I looked back to see the bell tower, with its bell still in place, clearly outlined against the darkening valley.

When I returned to Batopilas, the entire town was in a festive mood. People were happy and dancing in the streets. Everyone had a smile and cheerful greeting. The wiring for the new electrical system was nearing completion, and rumors were flying that the mine was to reopen. In fact, the electricity was provided by a large diesel engine placed outside the mine entrance. A passable one-lane road had been constructed from La Bufa to Batopilas four years earlier, and now the lights were going to be turned on! Truly a great event. They say that Batopilas was the second town in Mexico to receive electricity, after Mexico City itself.

I didn't realize what lay ahead for me. Anticipating the all-day rough ride to Creel, which would begin at 4 a.m., I went to bed early. Not long after, a small band which I had photographed earlier began to play their melodies. By midnight the festival had reached a crescendo – the band strolled through the town playing merry tunes. By 2 a.m. their music was rousing but unrecognizable. When I boarded the bus at 4 a.m., I could still hear them on the other side of town. They sounded like a little wind-up band with most of the spring-propelled energy wound out. They played slower and slower, but still with heart. I'm sure the music lasted until dawn.

The bus ride back to Creel was, to say the least, "rough." Within twenty minutes of leaving town, the short bus was totally packed with people standing chest-to-back in the aisle. Fortunately, I had a square-foot section of a seat and somehow managed to fall asleep. When I awoke at dawn, we were out of the canyon and grinding slowly up the road, surrounded by pines.

Looking back on the experience, several questions still haunt me. Did the early padres come down from the high mountains into the fantastically rugged canyons to found Satevó, or did they come up along the river from the adjacent unexplored lowlands to the west? Who and when are still points of historical interest, but why is really the outstanding question.

When I first saw Satevó, I didn't know how really unique the building was. First of all, the structure is huge. A large church in a major city would be hard-pressed to be its equal. Secondly, the complexity of design is noteworthy. Satevó has three domes - one large, one medium, and a small one atop the bell tower. It also has four half-domes and a vaulted ceiling. I am not an expert by any means, but having visited at least a dozen colonial missions, I don't remember any as being as large or as impressive. Certainly, none have been set in as spectacular or rugged a natural environment!

To get the proper perspective on the age and remote wilderness setting of the mission at Satevó, imagine how John Wesley Powell would have felt on August 16, 1869, as he explored Bright Angel Creek in the Grand Canyon and found the well-preserved ruins of a grand church complete with bell tower. Imagine today, hiking to Phantom Ranch and exploring a fantastic ruin built before the Declaration of Independence was signed. The impact is startling.

In the end, the spirit of Satevo is what impressed me the most. Some folks may see only a crumbling old ruin surrounded by a dusty desert valley. What I experienced was the canyon, the river, and the cathedral; it was beautiful and is still a compelling mystery.

When Visiting Batopilas,
The Lost Treasure Of The Sierra Madre

Many quaint colonial mining towns are scattered throughout the Sierra Madre. Alamos, Cosala, and Chínipas are just a few of these relics that evoke memories of a bygone era. These places are as rich with legend as they were with gold and silver. Stories of silver barons, lost Jesuit gold mines, banditos, Indian revolts, danger, and adventure abound in this mysterious mountain range.

The town of Batopilas glitters like a jewel, nestled deep in one of North America's deepest canyons. Breathtaking landscape, with a meandering emerald-green river and a year-round display of flowers, and the hospitality of the tranquil natives add to the ambiance of this colonial mining village rich with history and romantic lure.

After a dusty, hot, thrilling journey from Creel, a simple cool shower seems like a touch of heaven here in this different kind of Shangri-La.

Old West mystery novels, harlequin romances, and the reports of a crusty young anthropologist simultaneously come to life here. Judge for yourself as you peruse the material about the *Lost Cathedral.* Or visit this place of the past yourself, and tell me - what makes Batopilas so special for you?

Today Batopilas is experiencing an increase in tourist visitation due to the construction of the new road. Just last year the bridge was rebuilt and a retaining wall was constructed to protect the town from periodic floods which sweep down the river. The pace of life is still slow, which makes this beautiful riverside village of flowers, music, and friendly people an attractive respite from modern life. There is still not one TV in Batopilas, and I can say it was never missed.

When visiting Batopilas, I often stay with Monse Bustillos who keeps a small family-style hotel. Meals are provided with the room for about $5.00 a night. Monse also runs the Tarahumara Arts and Crafts Store, and is very familiar with the surrounding canyons and people. The capacity of her house is six to eight people, and she usually has a few people already in residence.

There are several other hotels in town. The Hotel Parador de la Montaña has a branch in Batopilas with a single room costing $12.00 and a double $15.00. This hotel is recommended for larger groups.

BASASEACHIC FALLS NATIONAL PARK

Long the subject of rumors and myths in Mexico's romantic Sierra Madre Mountains, Basaseachi Falls is today a reality to the modern adventure traveler. Truly one of the world's great waterfalls, Cascada de Basaseachi is without question the single most impressive land feature between the Grand Canyon of the Colorado and the volcanoes of south-central Mexico. The national park protects not only the great 806-foot falls, but at least five other cascades and one of the most spectacular canyons in the hemisphere. Recently made accessible by a well-maintained road, this natural area beckons to the adventurous explorer.

The only officially designated national park in the northern Sierra Madre, Basaseachi Falls represents one of Mexico's and the world's greatest natural treasures.

The name Basaseachi is Tarahumaran in origin, and means place of the cascade" or "of the coyotes." It is interesting to note that no Tarahumara word ends in a consonant. The "c" on the end of Basaseachic is added to Mexicanize the Indian word. I feel that it is appropriate that the falls itself be called Basaseachi, and the national park, Basaseachic. There are no Tarahumara living in this area today.

Carl Lumholtz reported in 1890 that the mining experts at Piños Altos measured the falls at 980 feet. Recently, the leading authority on Sierra Madre geography and climate, Robert H. Schmidt, Jr., Ph.D., measured the falls precisely at 806 ft. (246 m). This would make Basaseachi the twentieth highest waterfall in the world, fourth highest in North America, and the highest in Mexico.

Basaseachi is in an alpine area at an elevation of 6,600 ft. (2,000 m). This area receives an average of 25 inches (63.5 cm) of rainfall annually, of which 72 percent falls during the summer months. The flow over the falls ranges from one drop at a time in the plunge pool below during the driest years to 3,510 cfs at the highwater mark.

Basaseachic Falls National Park's first superintendent is Marta Carrillo. She has been stationed at the park for many years and loves the "muy pacífico" feeling of the area. Basaseachi has a distinctly spiritual and heavenly feeling surrounding the falls. It is appropriate that an angelic person such as Marta Carrillo should be the first guardian of the falls.

Ms. Carrillo strives to keep one of Mexico's natural treasures in its natural state, and to protect the park's flora and fauna. Despite her efforts, the park is now in critical danger on three different levels. First, the park area itself is not much bigger than the average city golf course. Slump-block housing and developments are pressing in on every side. The park boundaries must be expanded by purchasing private land surrounding the boundaries, and returning the land to its natural state. Secondly, tree cutting within the park continues (mostly for bridges that wash out with each flood); deforestation around the park boundaries has reached crisis proportions. The madroño, which frames the falls in this section, was recently cut down for firewood. A slump block house was built in the middle of the meadow. The third threat is really a culmination of various factors affecting Mexico as a whole. Overgrazing (in and around the park), deforestation, population pressure, and general lack of proper waste disposal systems will destroy the park (as we know it today) within the next five years. The general area around the park has deteriorated greatly from what it was in Carl Lumholtz's day, when the imperial woodpecker, the grizzly bear, and the wolverine lived throughout this area. Today, the Mexican people must make a decision. Allow the entire area to become a huge waste heap with dirty streams of water falling 806 ft. into a desert, or return the park and surrounding hills to their natural state of beauty and tranquility

Nowhere in the world has the decision to preserve a national park been easy or without conflict. Basaseachic National Park is one of Mexico's and the Earth's finest natural areas. This park stands as a challenge. Can and will the Mexican people decide for a better future?

The Trail To The Base Of The Falls

One of the most interesting and beautiful hikes in the Sierra Madre is to the base of Basaseachi Falls.

In the approximate center of the village of Basaseachi, turn south and travel down the gravel road to the parking lot near the top of the falls. At the parking lot, the trail continues southwest and crosses the Basaseachi Creek on an elevated bridge. From the bridge the trail winds through a pretty forest by the creek to the top of the falls.

Approximately 50 yards upstream of the falls, cross the stream again. At this point look for the trail climbing steeply up the east ridge to a saddle. At this low saddle the trail drops approximately 1,000 feet steeply to the base of the falls. Upon reaching the bottom, stay on the east side of the creek to reach the actual plunge pool below the falls.

The trail has been newly renovated (1986) and has steps in some areas. This is a fantastically beautiful hike. Allow ½ to 1 hour descent and 1½ hours ascent time.

Backpacking The Barrancas

General Information

I waited many years before planning my first major expedition into the heart of the Sierra Madre barranca country. Everything I had read or heard led me to believe that any backpacking adventure was doomed from the start to incredible hardship, danger, and probable disaster. I interviewed dozens of backpackers who had returned from expeditions into the canyons. They all told stories that were similar to magazine articles I had read. Most returning adventurers related the navigation was difficult, if not impossible, that there were many real hazards, and that none of them had been able to achieve their goals.

This last point was what really held me back. I didn't mind, as one writer put it, "plunging over a cliff and grabbing hold of a unique variety of poison ivy with thorns to save my life." I had had plenty of similar experiences in Arizona's canyons of the Mogollon Rim. A writer from a major national magazine wrote that he "had to slither under river side boulders like a snake, climb over slippery cliffs like a water spider, swim through long pools like a fish and hack through a cactus jungle like a safari guide with his bare hands." Another writer said that "the maps had been made by a pilot sketching with one hand while he peered between the clouds for a glimpse of the landscape below." These are good descriptions by professional writers (natural habitat - Northeastern U.S.) trying to perform the fine art of Canyoneering without training or practice. What really concerned me was that nobody was able to achieve their expedition objectives. I knew from experience that it was easy to waste two weeks wandering from goat pasture to goat pasture, or spending several days trying to get through a couple of miles of canyon bottom.

The canyon bottom contains the most spectacular scenery, so the best plans is to pack to the river by an established goat trail and day hike the narrows. If you want to explore two areas, twenty miles apart, it is easier to explore one area and return to the rim, then hike or get a ride around to the next area and descend once more into the canyon.

Unlike the mountains and canyons of the United States, people live all over the steep barranca country. Consequently, almost all trails lead to pastures for their livestock. Most travel in the barrancas is not from one scenic destination to another, but from home to pasture and pasture to pasture. Very few direct trails exist anywhere in the canyon country. However, a few major trails do exist in several areas, running from rim to rim.

Guides

Guides are sometimes available for backpacking trips. Local men will occasionally take a few days off to lead a group through the Sierras. There are no professional wilderness guides as there are in the U.S. or Nepal. If you hire a guide, remember that he is really a family man and a farmer. He may lead you for a couple of days, but soon his concern for his family will draw him home. He may not tell you that he is leaving. Several large parties have been left stranded deep in the mountains. These backpackers didn't understand that a responsible family man may not be a dependable guide. Should you hire a guide, I recommend that you have a short trip in mind and realize that your guide may not go all the way with you. You are also responsible for providing his food.

Seasons

Recommended season for backpacking trips is January through March, which is the cool, dry period of the year.

Rainfall and Temperature Charts for the Barrancas Country

Canyon Floor - Subtropical
Hot-wet summer
Warm-dry winter
Max. temp. 112 F°
Min. temp. 10 F°

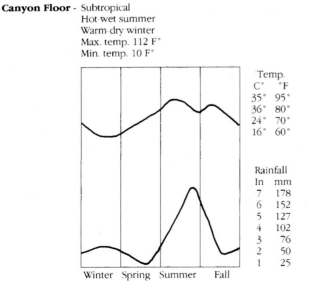

Temp.	
C°	°F
35°	95°
36°	80°
24°	70°
16°	60°

Rainfall	
In	mm
7	178
6	152
5	127
4	102
3	76
2	50
1	25

Canyon Rim - Alpine
Warm-wet summer
Cold-dry winter
Max. temp. 100 F°
Min. temp. -9 F°

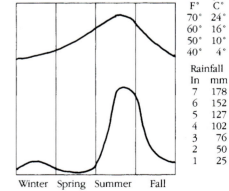

Temp.	
F°	C°
70°	24°
60°	16°
50°	10°
40°	4°

Rainfall	
In	mm
7	178
6	152
5	127
4	102
3	76
2	50
1	25

Maps

Barranca del Cobre – Barranca de Sinforosa
America's 1:250,000 San Juanito (1973) Hoja NG13-1
America's 1:250,000 Guachochi (1973) Hoja NG13-4

The Mystical Barrancas

Satevo – The Lost Cathedral

Tubares Mission – Rio Fuerte

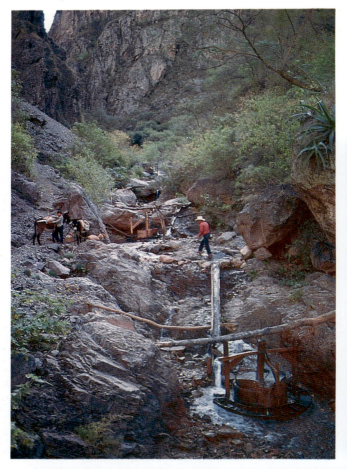

Ancient Mines of the Mystical Barrancas. *Silver, gold, copper – the treasures of the Sierra Madre are concentrated in the great canyons of Chihuahua. The mines are still occasionally worked with methods used a hundred years ago in Batopilas, La Bufa, Cerro Colorado, Urique, and Barranca del Cobre.*

Batopilas – *A lost treasure of the Sierra Madre. An experience in Mexican history and traditional culture. A "muy pacífico" pueblito of flowers by an emerald-green river.*

The many cultures of the Batopilas Canyon makes this one of the most fascinating places on earth.

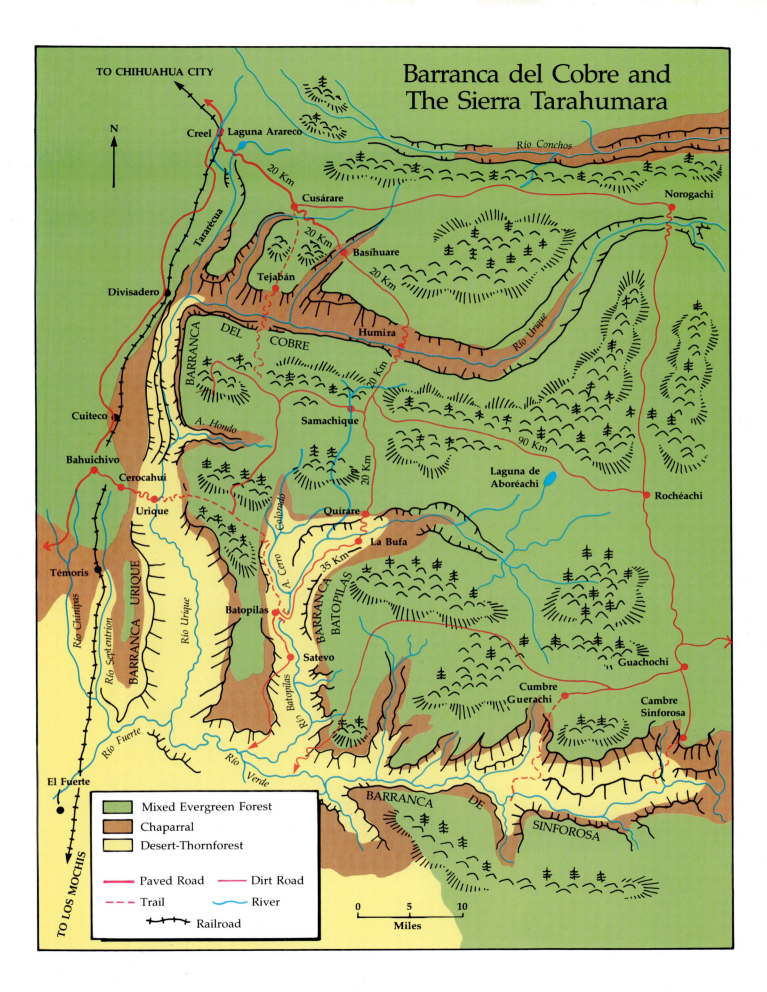

Barranca del Cobre and The Sierra Tarahumara

TO CHIHUAHUA CITY

N

Creel   Laguna Arareco

Río Conchos

Cusárare

Norogachi

20 Km

Tararécua

20 Km

Basíhuare

Tejabán

20 Km

Divisadero

BARRANCA

DEL   COBRE

Humira

Río Urique

20 Km

A. Hondo

Samachique

Cuiteco

90 Km

Bahuichivo

Cerocahui

Laguna de
Aboréachi

Urique

A. Cerro

Colorado

20 Km

Quírare

Rochéachi

La Bufa

Témoris

BARRANCA

URIQUE

Río Chinipas

Río Septentrión

Río Urique

35 Km

BARRANCA

BATOPILAS

Batopilas

Río Batopilas

Satevo

Guachochi

Cumbre
Guerachi

Cambre
Sinforosa

Río Fuerte

Río Verde

BARRANCA   DE

SINFOROSA

El Fuerte

	Legend
🟩	Mixed Evergreen Forest
🟫	Chaparral
🟨	Desert-Thornforest

TO LOS MOCHIS

——— Paved Road   ——— Dirt Road

- - - - Trail   ——— River

+++++ Railroad

0   5   10

Miles

Dos Colas Falls – Temoris

Coyachique Falls – Batopilas Canyon

The Narrows – Barranca de Sinforosa

Incised Meanders – Copper Canyon

First Descent – Upper Rio Conchos

Los Pilares – Upper Rio Conchos

Pastoral Life – Basaseachic Falls

Humira Narrows – Copper Canyon

Tarahumara Village – Batopilas Canyon

CAVE DWELLINGS OF THE HUAPOCA CANYON – MADERA
Courtesy of www.great-adventures.com

In early spring, pockets of snow shelter in the shadowed crevices of the high sierra. Brisk breezes, still carrying a tinge of winter's chill, bend the boughs of mighty pine trees and spread their fragrance throughout the forests of Madera. To the north of town, at the narrow chasm of Arroyo de Garabato, the sun casts its first light on streaked, salmon-colored cliffs that plunge to the river below. Here, the cave dwellings of Cuarenta Casas are tucked into the rocky overhangs of these massive walls. The Cuarenta Casas archaeological site is the most well known and accessible of the cave and cliff dwellings in northern Mexico. No one is sure why they were built but their location high above the river with an encompassing view of both the sierra and the canyon suggests that they may have been guard posts along an old trade route that linked Paquimé with the Pacific coast.

The great Paquimé culture flourished as the main trade and ceremonial center of northern Mexico around 1300 AD. Its trade routes extended to the Pacific, the Gulf of Mexico and to other cultural centers to the north such as Mesa Verde in Colorado and Chaco Canyon in New Mexico. The routes to the Pacific followed the Piedras Verdes River to the south and connected with the rivers that flow to the Pacific by way of smaller arroyos and canyons. Among these is the Huapoca Canyon to the west of the town of Madera. The Huapoca Canyon is not among the deepest of the Sierra Tarahumara but it possesses the most archaeological interest.

There are five main cave communities near Madera. To the north are **Cuarenta Casas** and **Cueva del Puente**. At the beginning of the sixteenth century, explorer Alvar Nunez Cabeza de Vaca wrote, "…and here by the side of the mountain, we forged our way inland more than 50 leagues and there found forty houses (cuarenta casas)." It is not certain if there were actually forty houses as fewer remain today. They can be viewed across the chasm from the visitor's hut and are not accessible to the public except for **Cueva de las Ventanas** which has some 1000-year-old Paquimé-style adobe dwellings with characteristic T-shaped doorways and stucco floors. Cueva de las Ventanas is larger than Cueva del Puente and they both require about an hour hike one way along a steep but well-maintained path.

Directly to the west of Madera are the **Anasazi caves** and **Cueva Grande**. Although they are fairly close on a map, poor roads and unkept trails make it difficult to visit both sites on a one-day trip. There are supposed to be guides available but this is not always the case so it is best for visitors to be accompanied by someone who knows the way. The Anasazi caves consist of the Cueva de la Serpiente and Nido del Aguila. Cueva de la Serpiente is the larger of the two with 14 adobe dwellings that are over a thousand years old. Nido del Aguila has only one dwelling that clings precariously to the edge of a sheer cliff under a rocky overhang that gives meaning to its name, the Eagle's Nest. The Anasazi caves are considered by some to be the most impressive of the cliff dwellings. This is due to the well-preserved structures, the integrity of the site itself which has not been as vandalized as other sites and the magnificent views high above the broad expanse of the Huapoca Canyon.

Across from the Anasazi caves, the descent from the sierra to the barranca is more gradual. **Cueva Grande** lies hidden within the convoluted folds of the land and is embraced by the branches of tall trees. The mouth of the cave is further obscured by a waterfall that cascades off the top of the cave to a pool and stream below. Even in drier months when the little waterfall is reduced to a trickle, the fine mist of water captures the sunlight to paint a delicate, shimmery rainbow. Its beauty, seclusion and constant water supply must have been idyllic to the people who lived in this parched, rugged terrain. A path rises from the pool to the cave's entrance just behind the waterfall. There are two 800 year old, two-story dwellings that provide good examples of the construction techniques of that time. There is also a round grain storage area behind the structure closest to the mouth of the cave.

The road forks just before crossing the suspension bridge at the bottom of the Huapoca Canyon on the way to Cueva Grande. The left fork descends to Agua Caliente de Huapoca, a small thermal spring on the riverbank. Its warm waters flow to a little soaking pool and continues on to the river where there is a natural swimming hole. Agua Caliente de Huapoca is reputed to cure a variety of ailments but it is perfect for sore feet after walking along the uneven trail to Cueva Grande.

It is difficult to find a taxi driver to make the trip to **La Ranchería** where there are some fine ruins that cover an extensive area at the base of the Sirupa Canyon. Located 50 Km south of Madera (a two-hour drive one way), there is a lengthy walk (another two hours each way) along a rough trail. A daytrip to La Ranchería requires a minimum of 9 to 10 hours with relatively little time to explore. The Sirupa Canyon is better visited on an overnight trip which also allows time to visit the site of the old San Andres de Sirupa Mission. It was destroyed during the Tarahumara uprising of 1690 and all that remains is the shell of a hacienda that was constructed there in 1830. However, the surrounding landscape is particularly beautiful and makes the half hour trip from the village of Sirupa worthwhile. Nearby, the thermal springs of Agua Caliente de Sirupa gush from the bank of the Sirupa River and is a good spot for camping.

Best Times to Go: Spring and fall have the best balance of cool sierras and warm barrancas. The beginning of fall is especially beautiful when the poplars and alders of Madera begin to change color.

Huapoca Canyon - Sirupa River Bridge

Getting There: Madera possesses a basic tourist infrastructure and is the closest town to the archaeological sites. It is reached from the nearby cities of Nuevo Casas Grandes, Cuauhtémoc and Chihuahua by local bus. See the "Getting There" section of the Sierra Tarahumara for general information about traveling to the Copper Canyon region from Mexican and U.S. cities.

By car, Madera is located to the south of Nuevo Casas Grandes and to the northwest of Chihuahua. There are two main routes from Ciudad Juárez. The longer but more interesting route follows Highway 2 westward to Janos then south to Nuevo Casas Grandes and Buenaventura. Take Route 28 to Gomez Farias and about 11 km out of town, watch the signs for the turnoff to Madera. The distance from Ciudad Juárez to Madera by this route is about 540 km. The other is to take the toll road to Chihuahua. Exit at El Sueco and travel to Buenaventura where Route 28 leads to Gomez Farias and Madera. This route from Ciudad Juárez to Madera is approximately 490 km.

From Chihuahua, take the Cuauhtémoc toll road (Highway 16) for 101 km to Cuauhtémoc and continue along Highway 16 to La Junta. Follow the signs to Guerrero, Matachi, Temosachi and on to Madera. The total distance from Chihuahua to Madera is about 285 km.

To visit the ruins, a good road leads to the Cuarenta Casas site and Cueva del Puente approximately 45 km to the north of Madera. Cueva Grande (66 km) and the Anasazi caves (33 km) are reached along a dirt road to the west from the roundabout at the entrance to Madera. Along this road just out of town, is the turnoff to the Sirupa Canyon region where the caves of the La Ranchería complex (50 km) are located.

Clothing/Gear: Substantial walking is required to visit the cave dwellings. Hiking boots are preferable for steep paths and loose scree especially in the rainy, summer months. Clothing should be comfortable and season appropriate. Remember that the sierras are cooler than the barrancas and even in summer months, a light jacket is needed. A flashlight is helpful for exploring the interior of the dwellings as well as the recesses of some caves. Within the canyons, bring a swimsuit and towel to take advantage of the refreshing rivers and thermal springs. All food and water must be carried into the canyon as no supplies are available outside of Madera.

General Information: Five main cave complexes are spread along the length of the Huapoca Canyon and its side canyons and arroyos. The distance between the sites, poor roads and the necessity of a one-to two-hour walk to each site makes it impractical to visit more than one complex in the course of a single day. An exception is the Cuarenta Casas site which can be combined with the Cueva del Puente. Both are located along the same paved road but an early start is recommended due to the requisite hike to the sites and back.

The best way to explore the Huapoca Canyon is by private 4WD vehicle with the option of camping when convenient. However, most visitors must make do with the limited tourist infrastructure of the region. Using Madera as a base, day trips can be undertaken to the cave dwellings. Tours are offered by the Motel Real del Bosque for groups of 4 to 6 depending on the destination. A more convenient alternative is to negotiate your own tour with a local taxi driver. The cost will vary but approximately $10 per hour is a reasonable rate.

The few hotels in Madera are more expensive than comparable hotels in Creel. The Motel Real del Bosque, located at the entrance to town, is considered to be the best hotel available and it has a good adjoining restaurant. Travelers arriving by bus may find the Parador de la Sierra and Motel Maria to be more convenient as they are located within walking distance of the bus station and other restaurants. Their facilities are not modern but rooms are clean with private bathrooms and hot water. Nearby grocery stores have a good variety of canned and fresh foods for picnic lunches and to supplement the mostly fried meals available in the restaurants. *Cave dwelling photography courtesy of Carlos Lazcano.*

Carlos Lazcano's beautiful new book "Exploration of Lost World's" is available through the Chihuahua Department of Tourism. 001-52-14-29-34-21 Chihuahua City, Mexico.

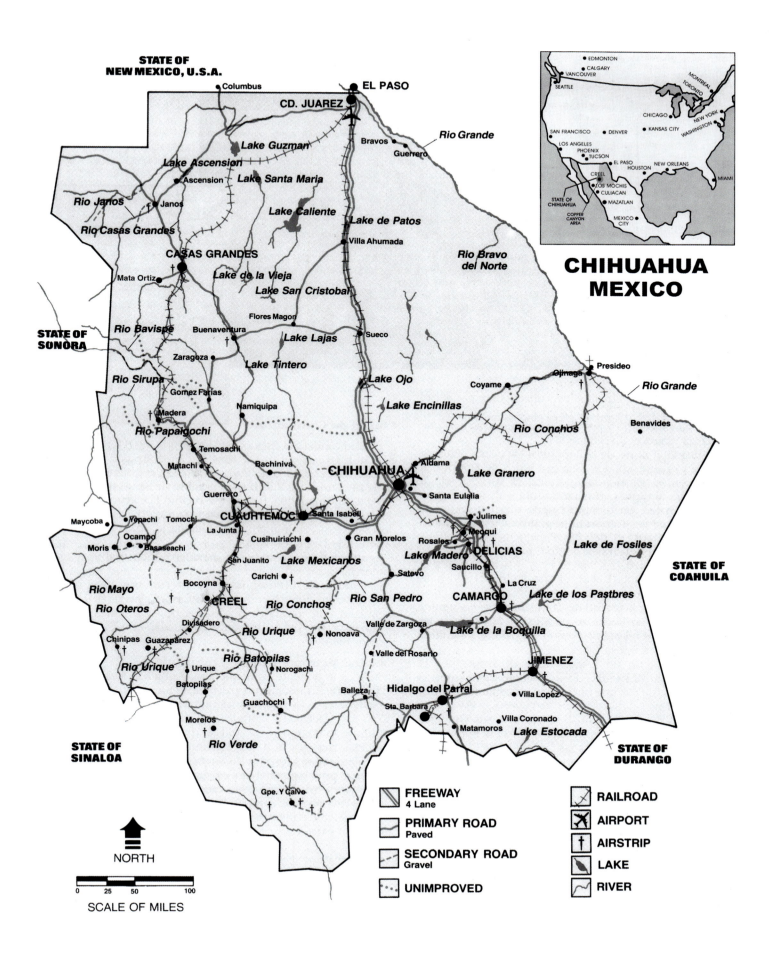

CHIHUAHUA MEXICO

STATE OF NEW MEXICO, U.S.A.

STATE OF SONORA

STATE OF SINALOA

STATE OF DURANGO

STATE OF COAHUILA

Columbus
EL PASO
CD. JUAREZ
Bravos
Guerrero
Rio Grande
Lake Guzman
Lake Ascension
Ascension
Lake Santa Maria
Rio Janos
Janos
Lake Caliente
Lake de Patos
Rio Casas Grandes
Villa Ahumada
CASAS GRANDES
Mata Ortiz
Lake de la Vieja
Rio Bravo del Norte
Lake San Cristobal
Flores Magon
Rio Bavispe
Buenaventura
Lake Lajas
Sueco
Zaragoza
Lake Tintero
Rio Sirupa
Lake Ojo
Presideo
Ojinaga
Coyame
Gomez Farias
Lake Encinillas
Rio Grande
Namiquipa
Madera
Rio Papaigochi
Rio Conchos
Benavides
Temosachi
Bachiniva
Matachi
Aldama
CHIHUAHUA
Lake Granero
Guerrero
Santa Eulalia
Maycoba
Yepachi
Tomochi
CUAUHTEMOC
Santa Isabell
Julimes
Ocampo
La Junta
Cusihuiriachi
Gran Morelos
Rosales
Meoqui
Lake de Fosiles
Moris
Basaseachi
San Juanito
Lake Mexicanos
Satevo
Lake Madero
DELICIAS
Carichi
Saucillo
Bocoyna
La Cruz
Rio Mayo
CREEL
Rio Conchos
Rio San Pedro
CAMARGO
Lake de los Pastbres
Rio Oteros
Divisadero
Rio Urique
Nonoava
Valle de Zargoza
Lake de la Boquilla
Chinipas
Guazaparez
Rio Batopilas
Valle del Rosario
Urique
Norogachi
JIMENEZ
Rio Urique
Batopilas
Villa Lopez
Guachochi
Balleza
Hidalgo del Parral
Morelos
Sta. Barbara
Villa Coronado
Rio Verde
Matamoros
Lake Estocada
Gpe. Y Calvo

NORTH

0 25 50 100
SCALE OF MILES

Legend

FREEWAY 4 Lane

PRIMARY ROAD Paved

SECONDARY ROAD Gravel

UNIMPROVED

RAILROAD

AIRPORT

AIRSTRIP

LAKE

RIVER

EDMONTON
CALGARY
VANCOUVER
SEATTLE
MONTREAL
TORONTO
CHICAGO
NEW YORK
SAN FRANCISCO
DENVER
KANSAS CITY
WASHINGTON
LOS ANGELES
PHOENIX
TUCSON
EL PASO
HOUSTON
NEW ORLEANS
MIAMI
CREEL
LOS MOCHIS
CULIACAN
STATE OF CHIHUAHUA
MAZATLAN
COPPER CANYON AREA
MEXICO CITY

Leaders for the Millennium

Juan Quezada's boyhood fascination with prehistoric pottery shards has led to a contemporary ceramic art movement now recognized in art circles from Mexico City to museums and galleries throughout the United States. Two generations of potters from the village of Mata Ortiz on the high plains of northern Chihuahua look to Juan as the originator and inspiration of their art form.

At 12 or 13, Juan began supplementing his family income by cutting wood in the mountains and hauling it back to Mata Ortiz on burros. As he crossed the plains, he picked up shards from the mounds left by the people of the prehistoric Casas Grandes culture. Intrigued by the beautiful designs and by the thought that the ancients had made such pottery, he began to search for clay and to experiment. Over a period of 15 years, he taught himself to make thin-walled pieces painted with intricate fine-lined designs. Through trial and error using his artistic skills, he recreated all of the steps of ceramic technology without any outside instruction or inspiration other than the shards. His work became a model for his relatives, then neighbors and friends of neighbors until now, 23 years after his discovery by an north American art historian, over 400 potters support their families by selling their wares to an ever-increasing number of traders and tourists.

To learn more about Juan Quezada and the potters of Mata Ortiz, read the "Miracle of Mata Ortiz" by Walter P. Parks which can be ordered from The Coulter Press • 6154 Hawarden Dr. • Riverside, CA 92506 • (909) 684-4224 for $19.95.

Carlos Lazcano Sahagún has been a leading explorer of Mexico for over 30 years. Initially drawn to the underground world of the great caves in central southern Mexico, his interest spread to include the entire country, particularly the northwestern region. He has been responsible for unusual and unexpected discoveries, primarily in the Baja California canyons and in the state of Chihuahua.

A good example of Lazcano's activity as an explorer is detailed in this book. He made numerous important discoveries in canyons of the northern part of the Sierra Tarahumara, in the state of Chihuahua. He discovered over 100 new archaeological sites of the little known Paquimé culture, the most important in the north of Mexico.

Lazcano, a geologist by training, graduated from the National University of Mexico (UNAM) and was a leading member of one of the most outstanding generations of explorers in UNAM's Mountaineering and Exploration Club. Lazcano has made exploration a way of life.

He is currently the director of Ecotourism Office of the state of Chihuahua. The author of several books on exploration, he has been a contributor to *Mexico Desconocido* magazine for over twenty years. He is also an outstanding photographer, much of his work having been published in newspapers, journals, and books throughout Mexico and internationally as well.

Carlos Lazcano's beautiful new book *"Exploration of Lost Worlds – Sites from the Period of the Paquimé Culture"* or *"Explorando Un Mundo Olvidado – Sitios Perdidos de la Cultura Paquimé"* is available through the Chihuahua Department of Tourism for approximately $50.00 USD. • 001-52-14-29-34-21 • Chihuahua City, Mexico.

Patrocinio Lopez, Tarahumara Master Carving Artist.

Patrocinio's violins are both noted for their fine workmanship and for their heads carved in the shapes of birds and animals. Like most true craftsmen, he seems the happiest when he is in his workshop making violins. He has won the national violin making championship in Creel six years in a row. Each year he and Richard D. Fisher sponsor a traditional dance group in the USA in the spring, where his violins are featured and much sought after.

The Tarahumara Indians, numbering about 40,000, have been called a nation of violinists. When the Spanish introduced the violin in the sixteenth century, the Tarahumara Indians fell in love with them and started making their own. In the evening a traveler can often hear Tarahumara violin music echoing through the canyons. Most of their religious celebrations are accompanied by violin music as well.

The Tarahumara, or Rarámuri, as they call themselves, live scattered in approximately 20,000 square miles of steep mountains and canyons in Mexico's Copper Canyon region. They are the last large group of native peoples in North America not assimilated by modern society. Living in small family groups, they have been able to subsist in harmony with their environment by growing corn, beans, and squash on the plateaus and flood plains of the deep canyons. These are a deeply spiritual people with a full and rich culture.

Patrocinio lives with his wife, five young daughters, and a new son "Ricardo" in a two-room house constructed of a combination of loosely fashioned materials – mostly hand-hewn timbers, adobe, stone, with a wood shake roof. Water is brought to the outside of the house by a small black plastic pipe which comes from a spring which is located a few hundred yards above his house. The closest road, electricity, or anything that would suggest that there is even a semi-modern world is a good half-days hike away. Patrocinio and his family live a very content, simple, country Native American lifestyle. Patrocinio's violins sell directly from him in the United States for approximately $200.00 USD.

ARCHAEOLOGICAL CIRCUIT
CASAS GRANDES – MADERA
Courtesy of Chihuahua Department Tourism

THE ARCHAEOLOGY CIRCUIT

The most important archaeological region of northern Mexico is found in the state of Chihuahua along the eastern foot of the Sierra Madre and nearby canyons. The vestiges of a great civilization that was established from the valleys of Casas Grandes to the lower slopes of the mountains near Madera serve as a window to Native American history. Here, over 900 years ago, the Mogollon culture achieved many architectural advances which are found in the great city of Paquimé and reflected in the constructions in natural caves such as Cuarenta Casas and Cueva Grande. The tours suggested provide an opportunity to witness the remains of a great culture which existed long before the arrival of the Spaniards.

THE ARCHAEOLOGY

A great number of important archaeological sites exist throughout the country of Mexico. Recent studies have defined the area in the central and southern parts of the country as Mesoamerica and the northern area as the Great Chichimeca. In most of the Mesoamerican regions, the cultural development was close enough to be called similar; suggesting that comparable processes began around the year 2000 B.C., with the establishment of stable agricultural settlements that, through the years, became civilizations and states.

The northern frontier of Mesoamerica was never stable of in its cultural development, primarily because of the diversity of the groups that inhabited the area. Additional factors were the adverse climate conditions in this desert region which resulted in extreme temperatures in both winter and summer months. The region is also very drought prone making permanent settlements difficult.

The first settlers to this region probably arrived about eleven thousand years ago. However, the earliest physical remains that have been located by archaeologists date to only about 6000 B.C. These people often lived in the land's natural caves. With the development of agricultural techniques, they began to settle along the riverbanks. The first settlers planted seeds from Mesoamerica such as corn, beans, squash, and cotton, making adaptations to the different weather conditions. As their techniques became more complex, the groups became less nomadic. The first villages were generally a group of small houses, known as fosses, with side entrances and roofs made out of sticks.

There are indications that by the year 700 A.D., the houses had become larger and there was an increase in the knowledge of agricultural techniques. Architectural change occurred, single dwellings gave way to housing complexes, some of which were five stories high. This is believed to have been due to an increased communications and cultural exchange with Mesoamerica (central and southern Mexico). Other similar housing facilities emerged at strategic points along the routes to what is currently called New Mexico and also the Sea of Cortés. Examples include Cuarenta Casas (40 houses), the Cueva Grande, and the Mogollon complex, among others. These buildings were similar in that they were constructed in natural caves and on impressive cliffs. In case of the Casas Grandes Valley, the Paquime site, a surprising discovery was the irrigation system which brought water to the city from a spring almost four miles to the north. This was accomplished by means of a narrow channel, terminating in a natural rock tank from which the water was distributed to a variety of areas within the complex.

Another interesting feature are the cages which were used to raise parrots. These birds were imported from the south of the country and their feathers were highly valued as adornments for ceremonial garb and for ritual customs. It seems the parrot may have had the same significance all over Mesoamerica and in the Great Chichimeca. It is believed that the birds represented water, rain, and fertility. Its image is frequently found on pottery specimens as well.

At some time during the fifteenth century, the city was suddenly abandoned. Archaeological evidence suggests the city of Paquimé was burned. Among the remains were ashes, various fallen walls, and a number of bodies which had not been properly buried. The reason is not fully understood even today. There may have been an internal rebellion of servants in their society or intense ritual warfare with neighboring pueblos over decreasing natural resources. Perhaps an attack by a hunter-gatherer tribe who wanted the food and wealth contained in the city was the final blow. A combination of all of the above seems most likely. No one knows for sure however. The most accepted hypothesis is that the destruction of Pacquimé was brought about by the Suma people, a tribe of hunter-gatherers. It was they who occupied the region when the Spanish first arrived almost two centuries later.

CASAS GRANDES — NUEVO CASAS GRANDES

The Casas Grandes Valley is divided by the Sierra Madre Occidental. Mountains, prairies, and deserts combine to form this beautiful land.

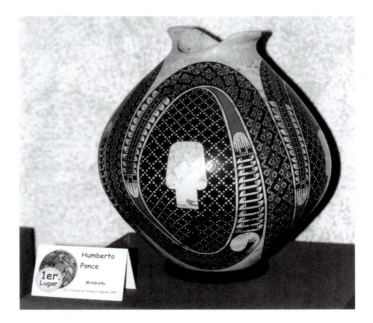

The first Spaniards arrived here in 1565. They were a part of an expedition from Durango led by Francisco de Ibarra. Baltazar de Obregón, the expedition's official historian, described the ruins as "a city that might have been constructed by the ancient Romans." The native people who lived in the area at the time were not the descendants of the architects of this great work, but it was from them that Obregón learned its name – Paquimé.

In 1661, the Franciscans began the process of converting the native population to Catholicism. They built a convent dedicated to San Antonio de Casas Grandes. The indigenous people did not accept Christianity easily and occasionally rebelled, though without much success. Settlements were built and were flourishing by the end of the nineteenth century and the beginning of the twentieth century, with the conquest of the Apaches and the coming of the railroad. Industries such as timber and mining arrived and developed the area economically. In 1875, the first Mormon pioneers arrived and settled in the area. With the arrival of the railroad, a new community was formed named Nuevo Casas Grandes. It remains the economic support to the original village. During the 1960s many more Mennonite immigrants arrived and adopted the land as their own.

Location and How to Get There: Casas Grandes is located 200 miles northwest of Chihuahua City and 100 miles southwest of Ciudad Juárez, in the Mexican State of Chihuahua. At an altitude of 4,760 feet above sea level, its temperature ranges from a low of about 14 degrees F in the winter to a high of about 95 degrees F in the summer. Some of the major points of interest in the area are as follows:

Paquimé. Located in the beautiful valley of Casas Grandes, Paquimé is the most important archaeological site in northern Mexico. This prehispanic city flourished between the 900 and 1300 AD with an astounding level of urbanization. The city was abandoned nearly two hundred years before the arrival of the first Spaniard, the evidence left behind suggested a very high level of civilization. Some of the buildings had as many as four levels and interior stairs. The site is characterized by its doors with the shape of a "T" and a very sophisticated – for the time – interior system of fresh water distribution. And it was the artisans here who developed the beautiful pottery for which this area is still renowned.

Museum of Northern Cultures. This jewel of a museum was recently constructed by the National Institute of Anthropology and History. Here, aided by many original pieces, models, illustrations, and videos, the visitor can learn much about the area's inhabitants over the various eras. This is one of the most advanced museums in all of Mexico.

Dublan and Juárez Mormon Colonies. These colonies were founded by immigrants who left the United States for religious reasons during the late 1800s. They held tight to their old traditions, as is apparent by their typical American-style homes.

El Capulin Mennonite Colony. This colony is inhabited by the decendants of Canadian Mennonites who settled here at the turn of the twentieth century. They are known for

their strong work ethic and are widely considered to be among the best farmers in the world. This group has clung more fiercely to their old traditions than the group who settled in the area of Cuauhtémoc, near the center of the state. To this day they do not use motor vehicles or listen to the radio.

Hacienda San Diego. Located about 16 miles south of Casas Grandes, the Hacienda San Diego was constructed in 1902 and remains well preserved. It was one of 30 haciendas that once belonged to Luis Terrazas, the biggest land baron that Chihuahua, and probably Mexico, has ever known.

Juan Mata Ortiz. Without a doubt, the most important artistic center in northern Mexico, Mata Ortiz is located just 34 miles south of Casas Grandes. It offers the visitor an opportunity to witness pottery making using the most ancient techniques. This is home to Juan Quezada who brought international recognition to his town through his talent and willingness to share his techniques for making the unique polychrome pieces with the people of his village.

SUGGESTED TOURS AROUND THE CASAS GRANDES VALLEY

Mormons and Mennonites: For a combination of these two cultures, you might begin with a visit to the Dublan Colony. Following a tour of the wonderful old wooden houses in the neighborhood, take the opportunity to dine in one that has been converted into a fine restaurant. A drive to the north just less than 20 miles, will bring you to El Capulin, the Mennonite colony. Here you will see evidence of the farmers' hard work as well as their unique lifestyle. (This tour lasts about 90 minutes.)

The Artisans from Mata Ortiz: This tour begins in Casas Grandes and heads south to the oldest Mormon Colony, Juarez Colony, which is home to one of the most prestigious schools in the area, the Juárez Academy. If you are fortunate enough to be making this trip in the spring, you will find yourself surrounded by thousands of fragrant apple and peach blossoms. Through the years, this region has developed into one of the country's finest fruit growing areas. A little over six miles south of Juarez Colony, you will see the Hacienda San Diego. Its turn-of-the-century construction merits at least a momentary stop. Just 3 miles further south along the same road, you will reach a little village names after a famous Mexican war hero, Juan Mata Ortiz. Within the walls of the old adobe houses of this village, the residents are creating some of the most beautiful and famous pieces of art in all of Mexico. With a little luck, you may be invited inside to witness the process. (This tour takes about 3 hours.)

Cueva de la Olla – Valle de las Cuevas: For this tour you will need a full day and the site is ideal for a picnic. Located 34 miles southwest of Casas Grandes, this natural cave contains vestiges of a civilization even older than that of Paquimé. In this unique cave is an enormous pot approximately 15 feet tall which was used for storing the community's grain. (It is recommended that you hire a local guide for this tour.)

Other Points of Interest: Cañon de los Monos offers a spectacle of petroglyphic art in a small canyon teeming with beautiful desert vegetation. (This tour takes about two hours.)

MADERA

Madera is located to the north of the Sierra Madre Occidental, in the northwestern part of the state of Chihuahua. Here you will find plains, canyons, and gorges, surrounded by forests of pine and oak. Here too, with the Papigochi River (also known locally as the Sirupa or Huapoca) is found the beginnings of one of the world's largest canyon systems.

A Brief History. The area around Madera was inhabited for at least the last 2000 years. The ruins found here served as dwellings for diverse ethnic groups, even different from the ones that formed the Paquimé culture. When the Spaniards first arrived here, it was inhabited by the Java Indians. However, they were not the decendants of the people that developed the great civilization that left a testimony to their existence in the caves and gorges.

The first Jesuit missionaries arrived at the end of the seventeenth century and founded the Nahuerachi and Sirupa centers. Both were destroyed during a rebellion by the natives which occurred in 1690. Around 1728, the first mines were discovered near Guaynopa which effectively began the process of colonization. In the early 1900s, the first sawmills were opened near a place called Ciénega San Pedro, which later became known as San Pedro Madera. An American by the name of William C. Green had the concession of a sawmill and he went on to create the Sierra Madre Land and Lumber Company which provided a great economic boost to the region. In 1906, the railroad began to serve the region.

Location. Madera is located 235 miles from Ciudad Juarez and is reached after first passing through Casas Grandes. It is some 173 miles northwest of Chihuahua City. At an elevation of 6,929 feet, its temperature ranges from winter lows of about 10 degrees F to summer highs of about 86 degrees.

Tourist Points of Interest. This is a region of many natural wonders and diverse archaeological sites with well-preserved dwellings built in natural caves and deep gorges.

SUGGESTED TOURS AROUND THE CITY OF MADERA

Archaeology and Scenery: This tour begins with a visit to the Peñitas Dam. In winter, migrating birds provide a colorful natural spectacle and, during the summer, it is a popular spot for fishing or boating tours. Follow the same road north for 26 miles and take the junction to the left to arrive at the archaeological site of Cuarenta Casas. A visit to the actual site requires a one-mile walk through a pleasant forest. (This tour takes about three hours.)

Archaeology and Nature: This tour begins on a dirt road through a forest just on the foothills of the Sierra Madre Occidental. The first place to visit is the Mogollon complex which includes the Cueva de la Serpiente and the Nido de Aguila, both of which are situated on high cliffs. From here, travel 19 miles to the west to a place known as Cueva Grande. This enormous natural cave contains a series of constructions. The final stop on this tour is the thermal waters of Huapoca. Here pleasant baths can be taken in natural pools. This can be a very welcome break after the rigors of visiting all the archaeological sites suggested above.

Sirupa Hot Springs: One of the most beautiful hot springs in the area, the water flows from three outlets in the earth, forming a small waterfall and pools that are just right for a comforting bath. Sirupa is located some 38 miles south of Madera and is reached by a dirt road. (This tour will last approximately four hours.)

El Tascate Fishing Club: An ideal site for fishing, boating, or camping, El Tascate is located only 20 minutes northeast of Madera.

Other Points of Interest: The Nahuerachi Hacienda is located just six miles southwest of Madera. It dates from the end of the seventeenth century when a mission by the same name was founded. The building is now in ruins, but it provides a glimpse of how the first Spanish settlements began. In 1690, this was the site of a bloody indigenous rebellion. If you continue along this road for another 13 miles to the south, you will come to the Tres Ojitos Mission. Here, the friendly priest and spiritual guide of the village, Jesus Espronceda, is a source of great information, historical and otherwise. He has even developed a local industry, teaching the people to make pork sausage the Spanish way.

Note: Archaeological site visiting hours are from 9:00 a.m. until 4:00 p.m., seven days a week. When possible, morning visits are recommended.

Paquimé – A Link Between Mesoamerica and the Pueblo World

by Silvia Marinas-Feliner

Many Americans have visited the great ancestral *Pueblo* sites in the United States such as Chaco Canyon in New Mexico, Mesa Verde in Colorado and Canyon de Chelly in Arizona. However, just south of the border in the Mexican state of Chihuahua lies perhaps *the* most interesting Pueblo site, the *Casas Grandes* (Spanish for "great houses"), also known as Paquimé. Paquimé is a Pueblo ruin that may have housed 2,000 or more persons until it was abandoned sometime in the late fifteenth or early sixteenth century. During the 1960s the pueblo was excavated almost exclusively under the direction of the late Dr. Charles DiPeso of the Amerind Foundation. DiPeso's published work on Paquimé is still an anthropology classic, a truly monumental piece of work. In recent years, the Mexican government has extensively restored Paquimé, and there is now a beautiful museum at the site, though most of Paquimé remains buried.

The most interesting thing about Paquimé, however, is not its large adobe building complex (originally up to four stories high with some original beams still in place) nor the wonderful restorations that have been done nor the fine collection of artifacts exhibited in the museum. Rather Paquimé, unlike Pueblo ruins in the United States, has numerous ceremonial mounds that, while crude in their construction, hint at the great temples of the famous Mesoamerican civilizations in central Mexico. For example, there are three mounds in the form of a snake, a cross and a bird, respectively. Also, Paquimé contains, at least, three ballcourts, one with its own large mound. DiPeso, in fact, believed that at one time Paquimé was taken over by or under the influence of Mesoamericans. With the advent of newer and more advanced research methods, most current researchers do not accept DiPeso's interpretation, but Paquimé as a possible link between the cultures of the southwestern United States and Mesoamerica has remained a hot item among researchers well into the 1990s.

The main method of house construction at Paquimé was a type of rammed-earth adobe, while the ceremonial mounds were made of soil enclosed with unfinished stone. There are no Pueblo-style kivas visible at the site

today, but there are still traces of the large, complex water supply system which supplied fresh running water to the houses and carried away sewage. The *paquimeños* had large reservoirs and an extensive irrigation system as well. Some of the rooms have the shapes of crosses, butterflies and other unusual shapes and there are a number of adobe "cages" used to raise parrots. There are many plazas at Paquimé and walking through the ruins with its many short, T-shaped doors gives one the feeling of being in a labyrinth. The level of complexity that existed at Paquimé before its demise is not known, though there is much evidence to suggest that its main role was that of a trade and/or ceremonial center rather than a seat of political power. Nor is it known exactly how Paquimé met its demise, though there is evidence of strife during its last years (around 1340 AD according to DiPeso, but estimates using newer techniques push the final dates closer to 1500 AD). Finally, where did the inhabitants go? There is some evidence to suggest that the present-day Tarahumaras of the Mexican Sierra Madre are related to Paquimé's inhabitants, but there are no definite conclusions.

Paquimé is easily reached by private vehicle over good roads. Or one can take a bus from most Mexican border cities to the large town of Nuevo Casas Grandes, the area's economic hub, and then take a local bus to the village of Casas Grandes. From the village one can easily walk to the ruins, though there is little in the way of accommodations. Most people stay and eat in Nuevo Casas Grandes. Paquimé is now a national park with most signs in English, Spanish and Tarahumara and has been recently selected as a UNESCO World Heritage Site. Finally, it is worthwhile to visit Paquimé both in the morning and in the afternoon as the lighting changes greatly with both time of day and with the seasons.

In addition to Paquimé, one can visit many related sites in Chihuahua such as the cliff dwellings at Cuarenta Casas (The 40 Houses) and at La Cueva de la Olla (Cave Valley) as well as the Arroyo de los Monos petroglyph site. Cave Valley has been severely looted but the setting is reminiscent in size and setting of the Gila Cliff Dwellings in southwestern New Mexico. Its large adobe grain storage vessel is very distinctive and there are many remnants of its once vast irrigation system. The Cuarenta Casas site is in overall better shape than Cueva de la Olla and is a bit more extensive.

FYI: Silvia Marinas-Feliner is an art conservator and restorer from Madrid, Spain with a specialization in archæology and archæological objects as well extensive experience restoring historical art objects. She recently finished her MA in anthropology; her thesis is entitled, "Paquimé: Architecture, Labor, and Sociopolitical Complexity." In addition to her field research at Paquimé, she has done Paleo-Indian surveys in Colorado and spent one summer working at the Ladder Ranch Mimbres Site near Hillsboro, New Mexico. She now resides in La Mesilla, New Mexico and is coordinating New Mexico State University's upcoming exhibition of nineteenth century Mexican *retablos* which will open in November in Las Cruces before touring Mexico and the United States.

The "Miracle" of Mata Ortiz Continues

by Jonathan E. "Jack" Davis

In the mid-1950s, a young man from the tiny Chihuahuan village of Juan Mata Ortiz began to experiment with making pottery in the prehistoric style of the Casas Grandes region. Juan Quezada Celado had found the pieces of many prehistoric pots as a boy and he knew the styles of the region well. But who could have guessed that this individual, with little formal education of any kind *and* holding down a variety of jobs to support a growing family, would discover not only how to mine clay and make natural pigments like the ancients, but also how to create exquisite pots that have sold for thousands of dollars! And because Juan Quezada taught his craft to almost anyone in the village who was interested, several hundred people, an entire village, now make their living from ceramics.

In 1976, anthropologist Spencer MacCallum discovered Juan Quezada's pots in a store in Deming, NM just north of the Mexican border. MacCallum soon went south in search of the maker, sure that he had discovered a true artist. After meeting Juan and gaining his confidence, MacCallum then provided a steady stream of financial support and encouragement to Juan for a number of years that allowed Juan the freedom to experiment with and Juan's hobby became his livelihood. By the time MacCallum decided his time had come to bow out gracefully in 1983, the village of Juan Mata Ortiz was well on its ways to discovery and economic development. During those "Spencer MacCallum" years, however, many El Paso-area residents like John and Marguerite Davis, Dr. G. Ken Burlingham, and Harold Naylor had become deeply dedicated to Mata Ortiz pottery. Through this network of aficionados, trips were soon being organized on an annual basis to bring more and more people to buy the beautiful pots.

In particular, the late John V. Davis of Deming, NM, became a mentor to many of the potters, especially the beginners. John's fascination with Mexico and the border region soon became a lifes dedication. For many years, up until his death in late 1998, John would visit Mata Ortiz often, sometimes three times a month. He was almost always available to put up a visitor for the night in Deming and then take the novice to share the experience of discovering the pottery of Mata Ortiz. John, a gentle cowboy at heart from the vast plains of southeastern Wyoming, had found a parallel world in Mata Ortiz. Prior to immersing himself in Mata Ortiz, the prehistoric rock art of Mexico and the Southwest was John's passion and his collection of rock art photographs numbers in the thousands. So when visiting the village, Juan Quezada would stop his work to take John to new rock art sites. Over the years, John's collections of Mata Ortiz pottery grew, to over 700 works of art, including six

early Juan Quezada pieces and the very first work of Juan's eldest son, Noe, considered by some to be Juan's artistic heir. But John's collection also contains many first works of potters who are yet to or who may never become well known as well as representative pieces from most of the village's senior artists.

No one could have foreseen these events that were yet to come when Spencer MacCallum discovered the first Juan Quezada pot...much less believed the events that had already transpired. Juan, after all, had begun to experiment with pottery in the 1950s. But he turned out to be a natural born inventor, an exquisite painter, a detail-oriented technician, an imaginative stylist, a superb teacher...and a great friend to many. Perhaps this last trait is what endeared him to people like John along with the cowboy heritage they shared. Juan soon began to teach the other members of his family, and then non-family members as well, how to make pots. At present, making and selling exquisite pottery is the lifeblood for practically everyone in the village of Mata Ortiz, over 300 persons in all. There are several excellent publications on Mata Ortiz by Walter Parks, Rick Cahill, and others.

Success hasn't changed the villagers all that much. Sure, there is a new air of "prosperity" as the once crumbling houses are refurbished. But adobe is still the building material of choice, and the village is still a very humble place that anyone can visit. Whenever a car with U.S. license plates enters the village, the visitors are almost immediately spotted and led by kids to the houses of the various potters. Being able to speak Spanish is nice; you'll be able to sit at the kitchen and converse with your hosts. But it's not really necessary if you want to buy pottery; the villagers are used to dealing with non-Spanish speakers. One is sure to see pottery in the various stages of design or painting, and with luck, see a firing under cow manure that has been dried to just the right moisture content. And for the truly interested, Juan has now taught numerous pottery courses in both the United States and Mexico. Juan Quezada, with the help of many, has created a wonderful legacy both for his village as well as for the world of modern art.

FYI: Jonathan E. "Jack" Davis, an El Paso native, holds a Ph.D. in horticulture/forestry, but these days he specializes in southwestern ecology and conservation issues. Although Jack is from the deserts of west Texas, he spent a lot of his youth studying forestry in east Texas and traveling the Rockies between his grandparents' Wyoming home and the rain forests of Costa Rica. La Mesilla, New Mexico is currently his home. He teaches part-time and is a private environmental sciences consultant.

REFLECTIONS ON JUAN QUEZADA CELADO—THE MAN AND THE ARTIST
RECIPIENT OF THE 1999 NATIONAL PRIZE OF SCIENCES AND ARTS

by Spencer Heath MacCallum

For many years Juan Quezada's work was better known in the United States and Europe than it was in Mexico. That has now changed. As recipient of the Premio Nacional de Ciencias y Artes, Mr. Quezada now has the very wonderful satisfaction of his art being fully recognized by his own countrymen.

The Premio Nacional is a fitting acknowledgment of an extraordinary talent and a rare human being. It is not yet clear whether Juan Quezada will be remembered primarily as an artist, a technologist, or a teacher. He is all three of these. His art is now recognized, but he deserves recognition as well for his extraordinarily experimental mind and his role as an inspired teacher.

It is no exaggeration to say that Juan Quezada has a truly renaissance stature as an artist. Often I am given credit for being the first person who recognized his genius. But I was not the first–not quite.

Some months before I met Juan early in 1976, Bill Miles, professor of ceramics at New Mexico State University, Las Cruces, visited Mata Ortiz, met Juan and recognized that what he was doing was more than craft–that it was truly art. While Bill's teaching and family duties prevented him from following up on that contact, the circumstances of my life were more flexible. I was fortunate to be able to devote the next six years, full-time, to encouraging Juan to develop his art in directions of his own choosing. He took full advantage of the opportunity I offered, and as he did so, I gradually introduced him to the art world.

Bill Miles kept in touch with all that Juan was doing during this time. At the end of three years, in 1979, Juan had his first traveling exhibition in the United States. Bill Miles met with us in Deming, New Mexico, on the eve of our departure for the opening of that exhibition at California State University, Fullerton. He made an unforgettable observation. "I don't know of any artist," he said, "anywhere in the world, in any age, working in any medium, who in a comparable period of time advanced his art as far as Juan has advanced his–and the more remarkable for being entirely self-directed."

In addition to being an accomplished artist, Juan is a practical man and a generous neighbor, ever ready to assist the less fortunate in ways calculated to preserve their dignity and independence. He has been responsible in more ways than anyone will ever know for the economic turn-around of Mata Ortiz. From the start he insisted, with a vigor that sometimes bewildered those around him, that those learning pottery do quality work. Yes, he said, there is a ready market for cheap products, but the future of the village depends on quality–on each person doing the best that is in him.

For a number of years, however, only six people were learning pottery, and the village was economically depressed. One of Juan's many ideas was that tile manufacture might provide employment for unskilled people in the village, and together we made a long, investigative trip to visit a tile factory in Monterrey. As it turned out, that never was necessary. During the decade of the '80s, after a slow beginning, pottery making suddenly caught on and spread through the village like a grass fire. It had become evident to all in the village that with pottery virtually anyone could, if he chose, make a good living doing only the very best of which he was capable.

Here is the magic and the riddle of the Mata Ortiz phenomenon: how could so much world-class artistic talent blossom from such a small, almost random sampling of population as that represented by this village? This is the puzzle that I think will occupy some of our best minds in coming decades. What does the experience of Mata Ortiz tell us about the creative potential latent in human nature? From the first day I met Juan Quezada, I felt an immediate, intuitive certainty that he had the potential to become known worldwide for his art, and I wanted to have a hand in bringing about the conditions that would be conducive to the flowering of that talent. What I never suspected–had no inkling of–was that all the village would become deeply involved, that within 20 years scarcely a family in the village would be without one or more potters producing world-class art. This is a magical happening, and it is the shadow of one man who, as a boy cutting wood on the hills above his village, became inspired by fragments of prehistoric pottery. He trusted the dream within him that he too could make such beauty. Experimenting alone for 15 years, he finally succeeded in re-creating de novo a ceramic technology and extrapolating from potsherds a whole design tradition. The world is more beautiful as a result, and the Premio Nacional is a perfect, fitting recognition of that fact.

Juan's curiosity, experimentation and initiative did more than set an example that brought prosperity to a village. It established new standards for ceramic art. Yet despite the unprecedented level of artistry achieved, it is remarkable how Juan continues to experiment and grow. Mexico, we love you for the tribute you have paid to your native son, to beauty, to the mystery of human creativity.

For an in-depth monthly updated calendar on Mata Ortiz events on both sides of the border, contact Spencer MacCallum • P.O. Box 180 • Tonopah, NV 89049 • (775) 482-2038.

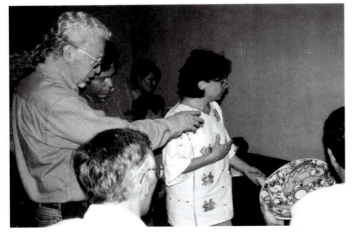

Judging pottery at the annual Mata Ortiz contest - 1999.

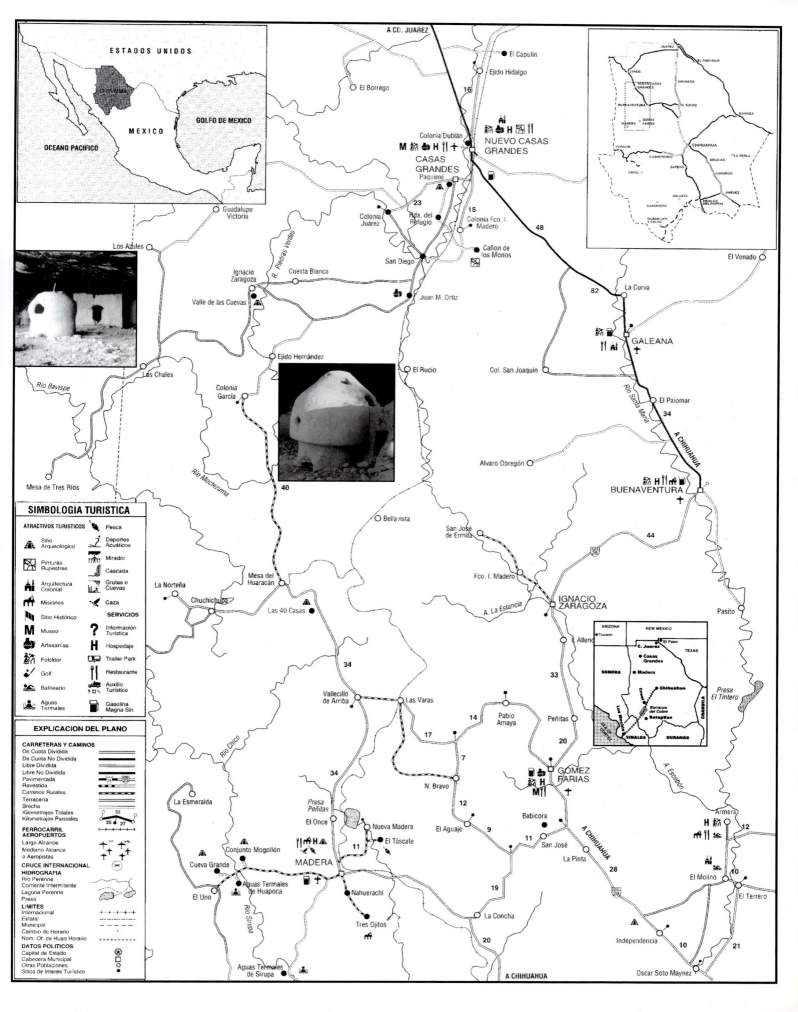

Map Labels

Insets (top left):
ESTADOS UNIDOS
CHIHUAHUA
MEXICO
GOLFO DE MEXICO
OCEANO PACIFICO

Inset (top right):
JUAREZ
EL PORVENIR
JANOS
AHUMADA
NUEVO CASAS GRANDES
EL SUECO
OJINAGA
BUENAVENTURA
GOMEZ FARIAS
MADERA
YEPACHI
CHIHUAHUA
LA PERLA
CUAUHTEMOC
SATEVO
DELICIAS
CREEL
CAMARGO
GUACHOCHI
BALLEZA
JIMENEZ
HIDALGO DEL PARRAL
GUADALUPE Y CALVO

Inset (lower right):
ARIZONA
NEW MEXICO
Tucson
El Paso
C. Juárez
TEXAS
SONORA
Casas Grandes
Madera
Chihuahua
Creel
Barranca del Cobre
Batopilas
Los Mochis
SINALOA
DURANGO
CHIHUAHUA
COAHUILA
Presa El Tintero

Main map place names:
A CD. JUAREZ
El Capulín
Ejido Hidalgo
16
El Borrego
Colonia Dublán
NUEVO CASAS GRANDES
CASAS GRANDES
Paquimé
Guadalupe Victoria
Colonia Juárez
Hda. del Refugio
Colonia Fco. I. Madero
23
15
48
Cañón de los Monos
El Venado
Los Azules
R. Piedras Verdes
Cuesta Blanca
San Diego
Ignacio Zaragoza
La Curva
82
Valle de las Cuevas
Juan M. Ortiz
GALEANA
Río Bavispe
Ejido Hernández
El Rucio
Col. San Joaquín
Río Santa María
El Palomar
34
Los Chales
Colonia García
A CHIHUAHUA
Mesa de Tres Ríos
Río Moctezuma
40
Alvaro Obregón
BUENAVENTURA
44
Bella Vista
San José de Ermita
La Norteña
Mesa del Huaracán
Fco. I. Madero
Pasito
Chuchichupa
Las 40 Casas
A. La Estancia
IGNACIO ZARAGOZA
34
I. Alleno
Río Chico
33
Vallecillo de Arriba
Las Varas
14
Pablo Amaya
Peñitas
17
20
7
La Esmeralda
34
N. Bravo
12
GOMEZ FARIAS
Presa Peñitas
El Once
Nueva Madera
El Táscate
El Aguaje
9
Babícora
Armera
Conjunto Mogollón
11
11
San José
H
Cueva Grande
MADERA
La Pinta
28
Aguas Termales de Huapoca
Nahuerachi
19
El Molino
El Uno
Río Sirupa
Tres Ojitos
La Concha
28
El Terrero
Aguas Termales de Sirupa
20
Independencia
10
21
Oscar Soto Maynez
A CHIHUAHUA

SIMBOLOGIA TURISTICA

ATRACTIVOS TURISTICOS

Sitio Arqueológico	Pesca
Pinturas Rupestres	Deportes Acuáticos
Arquitectura Colonial	Mirador
Misiones	Cascada
Sitio Histórico	Grutas o Cuevas
Museo	Caza
Artesanías	**SERVICIOS**
Folclor	Información Turística
Golf	Hospedaje
Balneario	Trailer Park
Aguas Termales	Restaurante
	Auxilio Turístico
	Gasolina Magna Sin

EXPLICACION DEL PLANO

CARRETERAS Y CAMINOS
De Cuota Dividida
De Cuota No Dividida
Libre Dividida
Libre No Dividida
Pavimentada
Revestida
Caminos Rurales
Terracería
Brecha
Kilometrajes Totales
Kilometrajes Parciales

FERROCARRIL
AEROPUERTOS
Largo Alcance
Mediano Alcance o Aeropistas

CRUCE INTERNACIONAL
HIDROGRAFIA
Río Perenne
Corriente Intermitente
Laguna Perenne
Presa

LIMITES
Internacional
Estatal
Municipal
Cambio de Horario
Nom. Of. de Huso Horario

DATOS POLITICOS
Capital de Estado
Cabecera Municipal
Otras Poblaciones
Sitios de Interés Turístico

COPPER CANYON

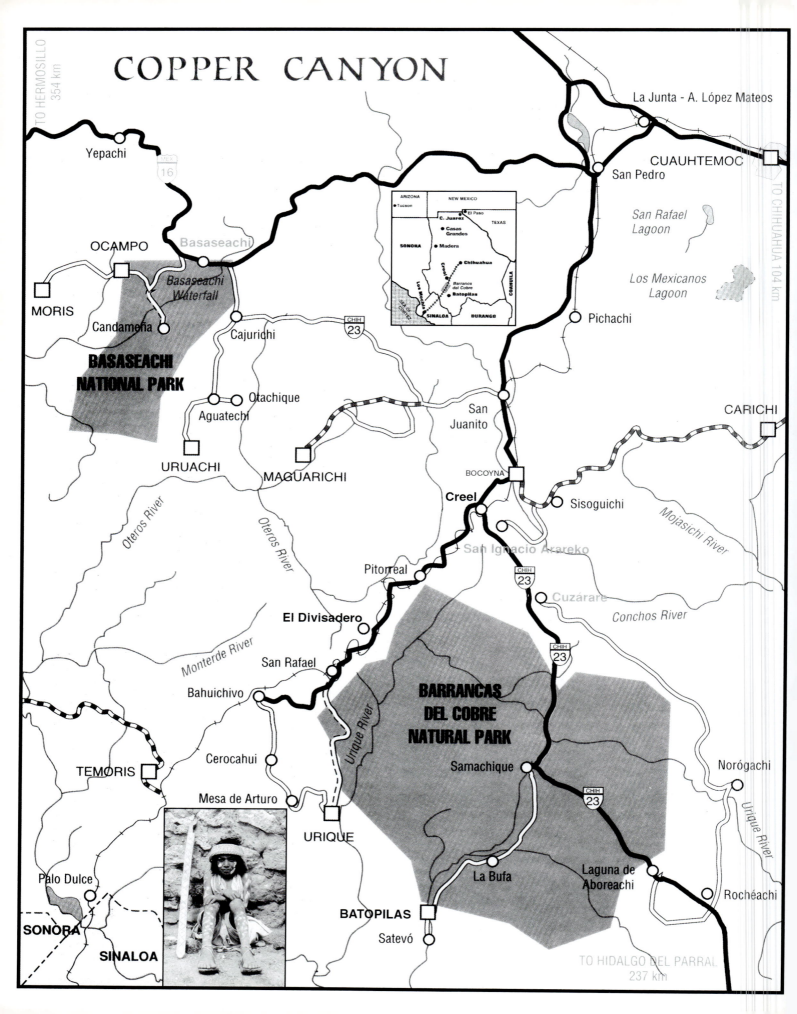

TO HERMOSILLO 354 km

Yepachi

MEX 16

OCAMPO

Basaseachi

Basaseachi Waterfall

MORIS

Candameña

Cajurichi

BASASEACHI NATIONAL PARK

Aguatechi

Otachique

URUACHI

MAGUARICHI

Oteros River

Oteros River

Monterde River

La Junta - A. López Mateos

CUAUHTEMOC

San Pedro

San Rafael Lagoon

Los Mexicanos Lagoon

Pichachi

CARICHI

CHIH 23

San Juanito

BOCOYNA

Creel

Sisoguichi

Mojasichi River

San Ignacio Arareko

CHIH 23

Cuzárare

Conchos River

Pitorreal

El Divisadero

San Rafael

Bahuichivo

BARRANCAS DEL COBRE NATURAL PARK

Urique River

Cerocahui

TEMORIS

Mesa de Arturo

URIQUE

Samachique

Norógachi

CHIH 23

Palo Dulce

SONORA

SINALOA

La Bufa

BATOPILAS

Satevó

Laguna de Aboreachi

Urique River

Rochéachi

TO HIDALGO DEL PARRAL 237 km

TO CHIHUAHUA 104 km

ARIZONA

NEW MEXICO

Tucson

El Paso

C. Juárez

TEXAS

Casas Grandes

SONORA

Madera

Chihuahua

Barranca del Cobre

COAHUILA

Los Mochis

Batopilas

SEA OF CORTEZ

SINALOA

DURANGO

BATOPILAS CANYON
Courtesy of www.great-adventures.com

Just beyond Kirare, the landscape suddenly unfolds to reveal the breathtaking expanse of the Batopilas Canyon. The lure of precious metals attracted the first visitors to this remote canyon but even the most avaricious treasure hunter would have interrupted his hurried journey to contemplate the magnificent panorama. Dizzying switchbacks descend a steep-sided canyon wall for 6,000 ft. (1,800 m) to a tiny bridge that crosses the silvered snake of the Batopilas River. Directly across the chasm, the Seven Steps rise precipitously toward the heavens. Perhaps it was here that Father Sun and Mother Moon of Tarahumara legend, descended to earth to bless their children.

From its headwaters near Tonachi, the Batopilas River winds along a tortuous, horseshoe shaped path to join the Río San Ignacio. Both the river and the canyon take their name from the seventeenth century mining town that was once renowned as a prodigious source of Mexican silver. Although Spanish *adelantados* (advance guards) discovered native silver glistening in the river in 1632 and attracted a small community of miners, the town of San Pedro de Batopilas was not established until 1709 when the Batopilas mines were discovered. Today the town is known only as Batopilas, a word derived from the Tarahumara '*bachotigori*' meaning 'near the river.'

Patracinio Lopez, master violin maker, at Semana Santa festival - 1997.

Accompanying the early miners and settlers were Jesuit missionaries who followed the section of El Camino Real that passed through the Batopilas Canyon. In 1745, *The Nuestra Señora de Loreto de Yoquivo Mission* was built in Yoquivo, now a small logging community located about 7.5 miles (12 kms) to the northeast of Batopilas. A circuitous trail passes from Satevo to Yoquivo and then to La Bufa or Batopilas before following the main road by the river back to Satevó. Signs mark the dirt road to Yoquivo from the main road before reaching Batopilas. However, inquiries must be made to locate the trails that lead from La Bufa and Satevó to Yoquivo. Although it is also possible to begin a hike in Yoquivo, transportation between the nearest town, Guachochi and Yoquivo is unreliable and it is difficult to organize a trek from Yoquivo which has few services. Still, the path between Yoquivo and La Bufa is quite scenic and a strenuous option for the determined trekker.

Very little is known about the *Santo Angel Custodio de Satevó Mission* because a fire destroyed its buildings and original parchment records in the late 1800s. Only the church, *Iglesia San Miguel de Satevó*, remains and is estimated to have been constructed between 1760 and 1764. Today, there are no Tarahumara living in the small community at Satevo but the size of the church and its location at the widest part of the Batopilas River indicate that it was once a fairly large Tarahumara community. Satevo is an easy 3.7 mile (6 km) walk from Batopilas along a graded dirt road that eventually comes to a bend where the glistening, whitewashed contours of the solitary church seem to materialize amidst the vastness of a wide, blue sky and the greenery of canyon walls interspersed with rocky outcroppings. There is a graceful, three-tiered bell tower but it cannot yet be seen because the structure blends with the surrounding red and ochre hills from which its bricks were made. On closer inspection, the church boasts 3 domes (a large main dome above the sanctuary, a medium-sized dome over the library that once connected the church with the monastery, and a small dome above the bell tower) and 4 half-domes that have all been plastered except for the bell tower dome. Some of the exterior walls have also been plastered but the original building was built entirely of fired brick and mortar. Bricks were molded, dried and fired on site while calspar taken from the silver mines was burned with river sand to make a durable limestone and sand mortar. Evidence of an oven for this purpose can still be seen to the side of the church. The process required large amounts of water for steam and children passing by carrying their water buckets remind us how little the rhythms of everyday life have changed deep in the barrancas.

Large wooden doors open to expose simple wooden benches on a stark stone floor. Wherever the pavement is uneven marks the presence of graves, some of which are inscribed with names and dates. Locals say that the unmarked grave at the very threshold of the church is that of an unnamed architect who fell to his death while placing the last brick in the church. However, one of the most interesting features of this church is the dominance of statues and portraits of the Virgin on the altar while the image of the Sacred Heart of Jesus sits unobtrusively to the side of the altar rather like an afterthought. The wall behind the altar is painted with blue pigment taken from a nearby copper mine but striated watermarks hint at an ongoing struggle with time and nature. There are other signs of

The author, Richard D. Fisher, exploring the Sierra Madre - 1986.

panies the river into town. It was constructed by Shepherd mainly to generate the hydroelectric power needed to light the mines and to operate the foundry that he built to eliminate the expense of shipping raw ore out of the canyon. Today, the aqueduct remains the town's source of water and electricity. It is an easy, pleasant walk along the 3.5 mile trail that follows the aqueduct to the old dam. Once a part of El Camino Real, there are sections where the original stone pavement can still be seen. The path passes some small farms growing fruits and vegetables as well as a few swimming holes in the river that are refreshing when water levels are safe. On arriving at the main bridge into town (also built by Shepherd), it is impossible not to notice the great stone wall that anchors a huge tescalama tree with sinuous roots weaving in and out of the stones. Beyond this wall is the ruin of Shepherd's adobe mansion, the Hacienda San Miguel. It is now densely overgrown with striking purple bougainvillea and a jumble of shrubs and bushes. Instead of using the main bridge to visit the mansion, most visitors like to cross the swaying footbridge providing much amusement to the more agile locals.

Although mining continues in Batopilas on a modest scale, the old mines now generate interest among travelers allowing the little town to capitalize on a growing industry in tourism. Many mines around Batopilas can be visited with some lovely views along the way. Across from the Hacienda San Miguel, a path leads steeply up the side of the canyon to the abandoned Penasquito silver mine. This 4.5

deterioration: faded wall drawings and inscriptions, crumbling brick arches and gaping cracks in the walls. Still, this old mission church stands with a compelling dignity offering the visitor a shaded respite from the scorching sun. In his book *The Silver Magnet* Grant Shepherd described his family's first picnic at Satevó where they encountered the remains of holy men strewn on the floor of the crypt located below the raised altar. It is not known if the vandals found the silver and gold that they were looking for but it is unlikely that they discovered one of its subtle treasures, its superb acoustics. A visit to the *Iglesias San Miguel de Satevo* is complete only when music fills the air, restoring the very soul of this lovely church.

The prolific mines of Batopilas Canyon have been the source of numerous personal fortunes. During the Spanish era, Don Angel Bustamante accumulated enough wealth to purchase a marquisate to become the Marquis de Batopilas. His local residence was the eighteenth century, La Casa Barffuson, one of the oldest buildings in Batopilas. The War of Independence from Spain brought about the expulsion of many Spaniards and mining production ceased for about 20 years. In the 1840s, Mexican Dona Natividad Ortiz and her associate Nepomuceno Avila reopened some of the closed mines and located several new veins. By the 1860s, the Americans began to arrive in Batopilas, the most notable being Alexander Shepherd, the last governor of Washington DC, who acquired his initial holdings in 1880. Much of Batopilas today reflects the work of this man who was responsible for the construction of most of the existing building and facilities.

The town of Batopilas is unusually placed along a narrow stretch of the river. It is three miles long and confined in width. To the north of Batopilas, a stone aqueduct accom-

La Bufa Canyon Bridge.

mile loop trail terminates at the southern part of the town. Another path starts at the south of Batopilas and enters a wide arroyo that forks to Arroyo Camuchin to the right and Arroyo Taunas to the left. Arroyo Camuchin is the gentler path that passes some small ranchos and through a thorn forest to the overgrown adobe ruins of a Camuchin community about 3 miles from town. Just beyond the ruins is the entrance to the Tescalama mine named for the unique fig tree at its entrance while across the arroyo, the Rosa Linda mine can be seen. Arroyo Taunas leads to a very scenic overlook after a steep climb out of the arroyo. Old mines can also be seen along this trail that requires 5 to 6 hrs. of hiking. A good variety of birds and butterflies are found in both arroyos and lesser long-nosed bats, *Leptonycteris curasoae,* live in many of the abandoned mines. Warm temperatures and the availability of food support large groups, especially in the summer months when the females gather in 'maternity colonies' where they give birth and raise their young.

Just beyond Kirare, Batopilas Canyon. Photo courtesy of Nathan P. Ervin – Pedro Palma Tours.

Some of the best views around Batopilas are found in Yerba Anise and Cerro Colorado, tiny villages high on the mesas above the town. The path to Yerba Anise begins at the trailhead across from the Hacienda San Miguel but continues steeply up the canyon past the turnoff to the Penasquito mine. This is a favorite hike for naturalists because birdlife and wildflowers are plentiful. Cerro Colorado is a small mining community that is about 5 hrs. walk from Batopilas. Some trekkers incorporate the Cerro Colorado hike into a multi-day trek to Urique or to El Tejaban. The trail begins to the north of town at Las Juntas just beyond the old dam. A newly graded road follows the Arroyo Cerro Colorado for about 2 hrs. before the road ascends steeply through oak forests. The little hamlet of Cerro Colorado is located on the mesa in the shadow of the peak bearing the same name. From Cerro Colorado, there are several trails to the town of Urique. The most direct passes up to Yesca and then down to Urique. A longer route follows the ridge between the Batopilas and Urique Canyons before dipping into the Urique Canyon where the trail alongside the river is taken northwards to Urique. These multi-day treks should only be attempted with the assistance of an experienced guide.

Best Times to Go: Exploring the Batopilas Canyon is best during the dry, cooler months of November to April. May is already quite hot and summer months bring rain and humidity. When planning a trip, remember that the rim can be very cold from December to February.

Getting There: Batopilas is most popularly accessed from Creel along a road that is paved all the way to Guachochi. At Samachique, about 44 miles (70 kms) from Creel, road signs indicate the turnoff to Batopilas. It is an unpaved road that passes through Kirare before descending the canyon to follow the river to the town of Batopilas 34 miles (55 kms.) away.

Buses depart from Creel to Batopilas on Tuesdays, Thursdays and Saturdays and return on Wednesdays, Fridays and Mondays. Hotels in Creel maintain current bus information and can also arrange for private transportation that may be more convenient.

Clothing/Gear: Warm weather clothing, good walking shoes, brimmed hat, insect repellent, and sunscreen are adequate for exploring the Batopilas area. In winter months, bring a light sweater for cool evenings. Additionally, backcountry trekkers need backpacking gear, an emergency first aid kit, snake bite kit, compass, flashlight and water filter. Personal toiletries, batteries for flashlights and cameras and film are not available in Batopilas.

General Information: Most of the accommodations in Batopilas are very modest and there are only a handful of restaurants and eating places. Margarita (known for her hotels in Creel) is currently building a hotel/restaurant complex to the north of town that is expected to be open for guests by Summer 2000. There is one four star hotel, the now famous "Skip's" Riverside Lodge which is on a package with the Copper Canyon Lodge near Creel. Skip McWilliam's Copper Canyon Lodges are now legendary for their very high quality food and service. These reservations are prearranged only. You can make reservations at www.coppercanyonlodges.com. All hotels can help with hiring a guide or organizing an overnight trek.

Plan to be incommunicado during a visit to Batopilas. The public telephone does not always work and the postal service is unreliable. Also, there are no banks so travelers should have enough pesos or US dollars on hand for the duration of their visit as cash is required for all transactions.

Backpacking Destinations

Other areas of this guidebook cover, in a general way, some of the hikes listed below. They are listed here again due to their importance, along with some new areas. The following is a system of rating to describe difficulty. "A" – very difficult, challenging, "B" – moderately difficult and "C" – easy. Plus or minus indicates slight variations.

Once you have completed four or five of these trips, you will have enough experience to branch out on your own. This guidebook highlights dozens of other interesting areas with basic map and destination information, provided you study the material.

Hike #1 — Basaséachic Falls, rated "C"+. This is to the bottom of the falls and is detailed in the Basaséachic Falls N.P. section. Day hike — 4 hours round trip.

Hike #2 — Barranca del Cobre-Tejabán is the Divisadero (overlook) of the Copper Canyon proper. This hike is rated a "B"+ multi-day expedition. The hike begins near the sawmill in Cusárare and crosses several high ridges before reaching the site of Tejabán. Although not a difficult hike per se, crossing the mountainous terrain to the rim can be exasperating. There is a maze of logging roads and trails where one can easily get lost. Therefore, a guide is highly recommended. With topographical maps in hand, I failed to locate Tejabán on three separate attempts, so I hired a guide with a pack horse. It took one full day on foot to reach the rim, making all the correct turns.

On my second trip to this incredible scenic overlook, I took a 4x4 Chevy Blazer. Even with previous experience, I made some wrong turns but was able to backtrack and find the correct route. There are two very rugged stretches of "road" as the track descends the mountain to the mesa where a Tejabán village formerly was.

At one time there was a hotel on the rim. The very first guest left a fire burning in the stove when he went for a late afternoon hike. The hotel burned down and was never rebuilt. A former governor of Chihuahua also had a summer home situated there. Today there are only ruins.

Historically, there was a major underground copper mine at the bottom of the canyon below Tejabán. It is still worked by hand, extracting some gold and possibly silver. Several *mestizo* families live near the mine and exchange small nuggets of white gold for the essentials of life.

On the rim above are several Tarahumara families. Young men are occasionally available to act as guides. From Tejabán the trail begins as an abandoned 4x4 road, then turns into a trail about a mile down near the ruins of a cabin. This road starts off in a west-northwest direction, and the trail that begins near the cabin reverses direction towards the southeast. At this point the trail descends sharply in an incredibly steep series of unending switchbacks. A half-mile or so below the cabin ruins is a seep (purify all water). Another half-mile below the seep is a junction. The left turn is for brave pedestrians and the right fork is for brave mule trains. The left turn descends steeply to the mine site. Although I haven't taken the mule trail, I assume that it descends at a slightly less challenging rate. It reaches the river about a mile downstream from the mine.

At the river is an amazing array of manmade and natural features. The details will be kept for your exploration and to the personal satisfaction of discovery. Plan to spend at least two nights enjoying this unique section of canyon.

It is possible to hike up to the opposite rim and reach a road leading to Samachique. This is a lonely mesa with little traffic. If the entire hike is made from Cusárare to Samachique, you will have covered one of the most interesting sections of the Camino Real. This "royal road" was a route that was used to bring silver from Batopilas to Chihuahua City. It is by far one of the most intriguing backcountry areas in the Copper Canyon-Sierra de Tarahumara region.

It is approximately 16 miles from Cusárare to Tejabán, one mile more to the end of the road at the cabin ruins, and from there two miles to the bottom of the canyon.

Tejabán is lovely in September to November and March thru April. The copper mine area is ideal November to March. Remember that Tejabán on the rim is a cool to cold 7,000 ft. and the mine site a warm-to-hot 3,000 ft. All in all the best season for travel to the are is winter.

(Caution) Tejabán has no drinking water available during the dry season; I want to emphasize again that a local or experienced guide is highly recommended for this particular expedition.

Hike #3 — The Barranca de Sinforosa. Rated "A" it is accessible through the remote town of Guachochi. Upon arriving in Guachochi, I asked to be take to the Cumbres de Sinforosa. It cost twenty dollars in cab fare to travel the ten mile road to the canyon rim. The rim overlook was spectacular! The trail to the bottom was the steepest I had ever been on. This barranca is deeper than the Grand Canyon of the Colorado. I would have been well advised to make the descent in two days. On the floor of the canyon, I explored the small village of an abandoned silver mine. There are beautiful narrows both up and down stream, and two major side canyons, each with waterfalls several miles apart on either side of the trail.

Further information on the Sinforosa Canyon is available in the "Lost Cathedral" section of this guidebook. The best months are December to February.

Hike #4 — Batopilas to Satevó, rated "C". This easy day hike is described in the "Lost Cathedral" section. Be advised that the floor of the canyon can be very hot, so I often leave Batopilas before sunrise and return at dusk. I spend most of the day in the church or swimming and resting down by the river to keep cool. The best moths are late November through February.

Hike #5 — Batopilas to Cerro Colorado, rated "C" overnight. About two miles upstream of Batopilas at La Junta, the trail turns east up a major side canyon. This is the lower section of the old Camino Real from Batopilas to Chihuahua during the silver mining heydays. Several ruins and inhabited station houses can be seen along the trail. At the small village of Cerro Colorado, sodas and snacks can usually be purchased. It is possible to day hike from Batopilas to Cerro Colorado, but this is 12 hour round trip. I recommend a backpack up to Cerro Colorado and then day hike upstream. As with the Satevó hike, this is a winter-only trip.

Hike #6 — Batopilas to Urique, rated "A/B" overnight. This is probably the most famous hike in the barrancas country. It is not, however, one of my favorite trips. I feel that the time involved in this rugged trip is better spent elsewhere. The trail leaves the main canyon at La Junta, passes through Cerro Colorado, and turns toward the northwest over a high ridge which divides the Batopilas-Urique Canyons. The Tarahumara have been replaced by Mexicans along much of this route. I recommend a guide from Batopilas, as there is a maze of trails and options along this route. Although the trip can be made over two nights, I recommend planning for at least four nights, since it is necessary to spend one or two nights in Urique waiting for a ride out to the train. A mail supply truck leaves Urique twice a week for the train station of Bahuichivo. This backpack is primarily for those in search of exercise, because it has very few redeeming values.

Sierra Tarahumara

THE ART OF BEING TARAHUMARA
By Kit Williams

Nearly every adult Tarahumara is a craftsperson. They weave woolen blankets, though no rugs, of high quality. Their pottery, presently more functional that decorative, is firm and sturdy. With encouragement, some of their production could become an art form in the non-Indian market. Their baskets are lovely and utilitarian. The women are folk artists par excellence *with needle and embroidery thread. Their woven sashes and sewn blouses might in some circles be considered* haute couture. *Wood carvers have demonstrated their ingenuity by shaping whimsical little figures out of pine bark to sell to tourists who arrive in Creel or Divisadero.*

Bernard L. Fontana
Tarahumara
Where Night is the Day of the Moon, 1979

The simple beauty of Tarahumara crafts is reflective of their lifestyle in general. Traditionally, the Tarahumara have had to make virtually everything they used in their daily lives. This has changed somewhat in recent years with the advent of a more cash-based economy, but handmade items continue to make up the majority of the cooking utensils, musical instruments and clothing found in traditional communities. Life is difficult in the rugged Sierra and this is demonstrated by the largely utilitarian nature of these articles.

Two factors have contributed to an increased interest on the part of many Tarahumara in making and even expanding their offerings of craft items for sale. Recent years have brought devastating droughts to the Sierra Tarahumara which have made the traditional subsistence farming increasingly less viable as a total, or even primary, means of survival. As a result, many Tarahumara have been forced to leave home in order to find work. In these cases, they are generally not particularly well-treated, nor is the pay really adequate. The manufacture and sale of arts and crafts provides an attractive alternative to this scenario in that the Tarahumara may earn the needed cash while remaining in their own communities and working in a way that is both comfortable

Patrocieno Lopez — consistently the best Tarahumara violin maker.

to them and within their culture. The second factor that has worked to promote Tarahumara arts and crafts as an industry is an increased interest in and appreciation of Native American cultures on the part of tourists who are visiting the region. The recent popularity of the "Southwestern-style" in decorating has also been instrumental in creating a market for items such as these.

The possibilities certainly exist for expanding this industry in much in the same way as the Native Americans of the southwestern U.S. have done. Several groups have worked

hard to help the Tarahumara promote their arts and crafts. The Mission Store in Creel is one such entity. During particularly difficult times, they continued to purchase any item brought to them by a Tarahumara, even though they were already seriously over-stocked. And all for a good cause as the proceeds directly benefit the Children's Hospital. A state organization, the Coordinación Estatal de la Tarahumara, also began a program as a result of the devastating drought of 1994 whereby they purchase and resell arts and crafts.

Unfortunately, the demand for Tarahumara crafts also opened the door for unscrupulous traders and in some cases they have already seized upon the opportunity. The Tarahumara are generally very honest and trusting. I am aware of one case in which a trader collected large amounts of arts and crafts which he promised to display and sell in a store in Chihuahua City. Several Tarahumara men worked diligently to collect items from people in their villages and even delivered them to the trader. That was over two years ago and, to this date, there have been no payments made nor have the items been returned.

Tarahumara art generally breaks down into five major categories: basketry, pottery, weaving, woodworking and sewing and embroidery. Often, slight variations in style will distinguish an article as originating from a particular village or area in the Sierra.

Basketry Baskets serve many functions in a traditional Tarahumara household. A basket may be used to store corn, beans, embroidery floss, or any of a number of other things. As the floors of most Tarahumara homes are dirt, baskets help keep personal items organized and clean.

There are generally two types of baskets; the first and most common being made of beargrass or *sotol*. These are used constantly in everyday life. The second type of basket is

fashioned from pine needles and, not surprisingly, is most common in the higher elevations where pine trees are prevalent. These baskets are quite small and delicate. They are made primarily for sale to tourists.

The beargrass baskets are made in a variety of sizes and shapes. In the mountain country, the *"guari"* type is most commonly found. These baskets are usually a single weave and are round at the top and somewhat square, with four distinct corners, at the bottom. The *"petaca"* is traditional to the canyon regions. It is round with a lid and frequently double woven. As the baskets can be quite bulky, the *"guari,"* in particular, are often made in graduating sizes so they may be nested. There may be 20 or more baskets in such a group. The set of nested baskets can be quite lovely, with the numerous basket edges giving the appearance of a flower in bloom. Recently, I have noticed more creativity in terms of style. A few Tarahumara have even begun to fashion hats using the same materials and techniques as with baskets.

The baskets are all made by twill plaiting, which results in a diagonal design. The basketmaker uses only her hands and teeth to fashion the basket, although the leaves are sometimes run across a stone to dull their sharp edges before they are worked.

Our family has found the baskets nearly as useful as the Tarahumara have. A large *"petaca"* basket makes a wonderful sewing basket and the smaller variety will keep tortillas nice and warm on the table. *"Guari"* work well for storing onions and garlic, among other things.

Pottery Tarahumara pots or *"ollas"* are used for a variety of cooking purposes. An *"olla"* may be employed to cook beans, boil corn with lime for making tortillas, roasting corn for pinole, and, above all, for making the Tarahumara's traditional corn beer, tesguino. Slightly different sizes and shapes define the use of a particular *"olla."* For instance, a corn roasting pot will have a handle on the top and the

opening to the side. This way the corn may be continually shaken and stirred over the fire so it doesn't burn. A tesguino pot is large and sits upright, with a wide mouth. Tarahumara pottery, as with virtually everything they make, is simple and functional.

The first step in potterymaking is to gather the clay. This may require a trip of several miles. Once the clay has been obtained, it is ground on a stone metate and mixed with pottery shards that have also been ground on the metate. Water is then added to this mixture and it is kneaded until the right consistency is achieved. Then it is time to begin forming the piece. The base is formed first and the sides are built up using coils of clay. The *"olla"* is always shaped by hand, although a piece of gourd may be used to smooth and scrape away any roughness. After drying in the sun, a hot fire is made in a shallow pit and the pot is fired.

If the *"olla"* is being made for personal use, it is frequently not decorated, although a leather thong may be put around the outside to make it easier to carry. When a pot is decorated it is almost always white or buff on red or red on buff. The red paint is obtained from red ochre or hematite and applied with the fingers or by means of a feather or cloth-wrapped stick.

The simple beauty of these pots has made them increasingly sought-after as objet d'art in the American Southwest. I have seen them in galleries in places such as Santa Fe and Sedona selling for upwards of $200.00. Unfortunately, I'm sure the bulk of this amount goes to the middleman and I doubt the actual Tarahumara artist received more than a mere pittance.

Weaving When the Spanish arrived in the Sierra Tarahumara in the early 1600s it was reported that the Tarahumara women were excellent weavers, but all they had to work with

Canyon Tarahumara Family

Rio Conchos – Tarahumara Home

as a material was agave fiber. Thanks to the introduction of sheep by the Spanish, the Tarahumara had begun weaving clothing and blankets of wool by 1625, a tradition that continues today.

Wool blankets and sashes call *"fajas"* are the items most frequently woven. Smaller, brightly colored belts are also becoming popular, primarily for sales to tourists.

Blankets are made from homespun yarn, usually in the natural colors of dark brown and white. On occasion, a brightly colored commercial yarn will be purchased and integrated into the work as well. These blankets serve the very useful purpose of keeping people warm during the sometimes frigid winter months. As such, they are woven in a most ingenious open weave so that the air spaces provide additional insulation.

A broad horizontal loom is utilized for weaving blankets. It is usually set low to the ground in the shade (if possible) in the yard of the house. The weaver sits at the end to work. The finished product, which may take a month or more to complete, is very heavy and warm.

If you purchase a blanket directly from the weaver, you will almost certainly get an excellent buy. Once you get it home, however, you should not fail to give it a good treatment for moths or you may well find your treasure disappearing before your eyes. This is critical as the moths may invade your house and damage other valuable articles as well.

Sashes or *"fajas"* and belts are woven on a smaller version of the horizontal loom. They are usually much brighter in color than the blankets, more frequently utilizing the purchased commercial yarns. The *"fajas"* are long and wide, used by men to affix their loincloths and occasionally by women for their skirts. The *"faja"* is wrapped around the waist and tied in such a way as to leave two "tails" hanging down the back.

While they are striking when used in combination with a traditional Tarahumara costume, the *"fajas"* are too wide and too long to find much of a market with tourists. The ever-resourceful Tarahumara began weaving a shorter, more narrow variety, frequently out of a cheaper acrylic yarn, that they have been very successful in selling as tie belts.

Wood Carving Tarahumara men love to work with wood and have learned to fashion amazingly detailed items with what might be considered fairly crude tools. Wooden spoons, bowls, and figurines are all items which are commonly carved. The wooden ball used in the traditional kickball race has become increasingly popular as a collector's item following the remarkable performances of members of the Tarahumara Racing Team in the United States. Team members have learned there is money to be made in the U.S. by bringing their crafts to sell, particularly these hand-carved, baseball-size balls. Although the American runners are already

in awe of the Tarahumara's legendary running abilities, they are even more stunned to see the wooden balls that are kicked with bare toes in a Tarahumara race.

Musical instruments such as drums and violins are also made frequently for use in ceremonies and sometimes for sale. Drums are made from pieces of goatskin stretched over a wooden frame. They are used extensively during the Holy Week or *Semana Santa* festivities and may be purchased directly from the owner just afterwards. As drums are considered ceremonial items, they can be more difficult to find during other times of the year. Some areas of the Sierra are considered to be superior with regard to the quality of the drums produced. In general, the drums from the Basihuare area are well made and painted with more elaborate designs.

Violins were first introduced to the Tarahumara by the Spanish and have come to play an important role in Tarahumara music and celebrations. The violins are all carved by hand, a painstaking process. Recently, several artisans have begun taking violins into a new creative realm, adding intricately carved animal figures to the scroll of the instrument. If you purchase a Tarahumara violin, it is a good idea to apply several coats of Tung oil when you get it home to protect your investment.

Sewing and Embroidery
While Tarahumara clothing has not yet found much of a market for sales to the outside world, Tarahumara women fashion beautiful garments for their families' personal use. Brightly colored headbands and pleated full skirts, blouses and shirts are made from purchased cloth. This cloth is torn, often using their teeth, into the appropriate sizes and shapes and then sewn by hand. Men's loincloths are embroidered with colorful figures in the shapes of flowers and other designs. There is little more scenic than a traditionally dressed Tarahumara family walking along the road to town.

While not made from fabric, Tarahumara sandals, or *"huaraches,"* are gaining fame throughout the world. These sandals are fashioned from old tire tread and leather thong and are reputed to be very comfortable. They have frequently been worn by members of the Tarahumara Racing Team when winning international distance races, much to the consternation of the manufacturers of expensive American running shoes.

The Tarahumara are currently at a juncture not unlike that of the Native Americans in the southwestern United States at the turn of the century. Outside influences have made their traditional lifestyle increasingly difficult to maintain, although the Tarahumara's efforts to do so thus far have certainly proved more successful than their U.S. counterparts'. It may be said that the culture of the Tarahumara has been largely defined through their art. Now, perhaps, Tarahumara art will help to provide a means for maintaining their culture.

The Tarahumara Race for Cultural Survival

Text and Photos By Kit Williams

THE LEGEND

Kórima in Tarahumara means sharing, but it is more than just a word. The spirit of sharing and cooperation is an integral part of the lives of the Tarahumara people. Living in the rugged canyons of northern Mexico, the Tarahumara are considered to be among the most traditional native Americans in North America. Only *kórima* enables them to survive as subsistence farmers and only with *kórima* can they persevere in their legendary long distances races.

When Europeans first probed the Americas, explorers noted the great running prowess of the Indian tribes. Later, as the tribes were decimated by conquest and foreign disease, and currently with the invasion of modern roads and motor vehicles, almost all of the tribes have lost their running ability. Fortunately, guarded by the almost impenetrable canyon country of the northern Sierra Madre, the Tarahumara have survived physically, and have managed to maintain much of their culture into the present era. The Tarahumara continue to walk great distances on a weekly basis for required subsistence and for enjoyment. This endurance walking maintains their physical health and strength for long distance racing events.

Racing plays an important role in Tarahumara culture both socially and economically. Participants from several villages and their families gather for the event, which results in great economic exchange through hefty wagers that take place in conjunction with the race.

Two teams compete with each other, alternately kicking and chasing wooden balls around the race course until all members of one team have dropped from exhaustion or conceded. There are reports of races that continued for several days and nights.

Given tales of such extraordinary endurance, the idea of Tarahumara participation in international racing events is not new. In fact, two Tarahumara men ran the marathon in the 1968 Olympics in Mexico City. More recently, Richard Fisher, an explorer and author/photographer who has written several guidebooks on the Copper Canyon region, sponsored a team of Tarahumara racers in the 1992 Leadville Trail 100 in Colorado. The results in these and other attempts have been largely disappointing, prompting

some to speculate that perhaps the renowned Tarahumara talent for running, if ever true, had become one of the first casualties to their culture as the outside world began encroaching upon their land.

Logging and road building efforts in the Tarahumara homeland present a very real threat to the people's health and traditional lifestyle. The deforestation currently taking place in the canyon has already resulted in flooding and erosion of Tarahumara farmlands. Subsequently, the Tarahumara have not been able to survive on their traditional subsistence agriculture and increasingly have had to turn to alternative means of survival such as sale of their handicrafts and working in nearby towns.

Meanwhile, there appears to have been a resurgence of interest in racing by the Tarahumara in their homeland. Travelling with Fisher through the Batopilas Canyon, we heard it over and over again.

"We're racing again," declares Chico, who lives about an hour's walk from the road near the old mining town of La Bufa.

"The Tarahumara are running again. I was invited to a race...what an experience!" said Bob, an American who works as a guide for a hotel in Batopilas.

And when we mention our interest in racing, a *mestizo* shopkeeper hastens to inform us, "They're running again. For a time they haven't run much, but lately there have been several races held nearby."

Although it cannot be stated unequivocally that this is a direct result of the participation of the five members of the tribe in the Leadville Trail 100, Felipe Torres, one of the Leadville participants, tells us, "We've run more in the past two months than in the two preceding years!"

While few outsiders were aware of the situation, the tradition of racing had apparently dwindled to the point that young and middle-aged men had little experience with races in their lifetimes. Patrocinio Lopez, one of the most influential members of the village we visited, was initially hesitant when Fisher approached him with the suggestion that they hold a traditional race.

"We haven't run here in six or seven years," he said. "We will have to ask the people and see what they think."

The Tarahumara had experienced a near total crop failure and hunger was a very real problem. "If you provide the food for the race maybe they will be happy and will want to run," suggested Patrocinio. "And that is what I think," he asserted, using the phrase I have come to realize marks nearly every personal opinion uttered.

And so it was. Although interested, many expressed concern that they might not do it "right." While planning the first race held in the village for some time, Ramon Moreno asked Fisher, "How long do you want us to run?" and "Where should we make the course?"

"It's your race and your tradition," came the reply, "do it however you want."

Thus encouraged, the advice of the older men who might remember these things was sought and age began teaching youth the ways of the past, particularly with regard to racing. As a result, large and complicated races are again becoming commonplace.

THE TRADITIONAL RACE

A largeTarahumara race was held on their own land and in a traditional manner. A beautiful and moving event, it will remain indelibly etched in the minds and hearts of those fortunate enough to have witnessed it.

Thanks to our involvement with the delivery of several tons of corn and other foodstuffs for the race, our group received a warm welcome and was invited to attend. We six Americans or *chabochis* (the bearded ones), as the Tarahumara refer to both the white man and *mestizo,* were not prepared for the magnitude of what we were to experience.

Traditional Racing – Antonio Palma

The Beauty of Tarahumara Lifestyles

The Beauty of Tarahumara Festivals

For us it actually began a few days before the race when, together with several of our Tarahumara companions, we bumped along the rough road in the back of a truck transporting the bags of corn, beans, and *maseca* (cornmeal) to the river where they would be carried another three hours by burro to the race site.

The dust from the road mixed with cornmeal that was leaking from small holes that began appearing in the bags. Soon we were all covered with a thick gray powder. Perched on top of bags of corn, we tried to keep our balance as the truck lurched around the treacherous canyon curves.

"Es bonito," Antonio said to me as we rolled along.

"What?" I asked, not seeing anything in the immediate vicinity that was remotely pretty or nice.

"Todo esto," (all this), he replied, patting the bags of food.

A Tarahumara race really begins several weeks prior to the actual event. The two *cabeceros,* or team leaders for this race are Ronrico and Desidero. It is the responsibility of each to invite and encourage the best runners to compete on his team. The invitation process alone takes days as it is necessary for each to travel by foot over rugged terrain through the canyon to reach villages which may be located 20 or more miles away.

As the appointed day approaches, the level of excitement increases. Members of the community begin placing bets on their favorite team.

Race sites may vary, even within the same community, depending upon which fields are currently under cultivation and cannot be trampled. If necessary, a few of the men will clear and ready the race course several days prior to race day. This consists of removing any major obstacles; but the course will remain extremely rocky and rugged. The race course itself is a loop, ranging from approximately two to five kilometers.

Finally race day dawns. The runners, together with their families and friends, begin traveling toward the race site. Some will walk 20 miles that morning just to reach the site.

The hillsides are dotted with color as the brightly dressed people make their way over the trails. The men wear shirts in hues of turquoise, marigold, orange, emerald green, or white, and embroidered breechcloths or *tagoras*. Different areas of the canyon are distinguished by slightly varied styles of *tagora* and the type of embroidery displayed thereon. The women wear similar blouses, paired with long, full skirts. The clothes are all hand-sewn and directly descended in style from those of the Spanish conquistadors, complete with collarless necklines and billowy sleeves. As head coverings, the men often sport bright headbands, while the women usually prefer multicolored scarves, tied under the chin.

The Tarahumara are known for their beautiful weavings called *fajas,* which serve as belts for the men. Sometimes bells are attached to the back of these belts which serve as a sort of runner's "metronome." Runners' pounding feet keep pace to the jingle jangle of the bells before them.

Race Judge – Patricio

Of most interest to runners in the United States, however, would be their shoes. In our high-tech times of air and gel-filled soles, the Tarahumara are covering trails rivaling those of the most infamous U.S. trail runs wearing sandals. The *huaraches* (sandals) are made of a foot-sized piece of tire tread, held on by leather thong. Some of the runners who had been to Leadville still had the shoes that were purchased for them but, at least on familiar soil, the *huaraches* win out.

"These are strong," declares Felipe, pointing at his sandals, "They will make it better than shoes."

So that's it...and in their *huaraches* the Tarahumara cover miles and miles of rocky and treacherous trail without so much as a misstep.

The two teams gather at separate locations, usually at a team member's home. Activity at each reaches a fevered pitch as the children play and women grind corn on stone metates and work over open fires to hurriedly prepare tortillas, beans, coffee, and *pinole* for runners and spectators alike. *Pinole,* a corn meal mixture that is thinned with water, is traditionally used as the primary source of nutrition during the race.

As the runners gather to eat and generally prepare themselves for the race to come, an important aspect of pre-race activity consists of casting spells and hexes on the other team.

Older men come too. Their days as racers but distant memories, they now perform vital functions as coaches and "medicine men" for their respective teams.

The root of an agave cactus is roasted over the fire by one of the elders. He then carefully pulls apart the onion-like layers and uses a stone to pound them against a large rock. These layers, believed to contain medicinal properties, are soaked in water which is used to anoint the runners' bodies before the race begins. Later, it will be brushed on a tired runner's legs, poured over his head and upper body, or even consumed.

Patricio approaches us. *"Me recuerdas?"* he asks. "Do you remember me?"

Indeed we do, but not like this. Dressed from head to toe in brilliant white and very much in charge of the proceedings, he is resplendent!

We had first met him several days before in the town of Batopilas where we found him carrying two viga beams to sell. They weighed at least seventy-five pounds each and after carrying them the 20-plus miles to town, he looked like a tired old man. The very next day we ran into him again. With a large bag of flour purchased with his earnings, he was waiting at the river crossing for the rain-swollen torrent to subside. Patricio, like many of the Tarahumara, doesn't swim. He waited for several hours to no avail. Finally a couple of the younger men got on either side of him and, taking him by the arms, helped him across. Another transported the bag of flour. As we watched this procession make its way slowly and unsteadily through the swirling muddy water, the small man in the middle seemed very frail and vulnerable, nothing at all like the figure who now stood proudly before us.

"Yes," we told him, "we certainly do remember you. It's very good to see you here."

Another elder busies himself carving the traditional wooden balls or *bolas*. The wooden ball is central to Tarahumara racing, because it is the position of the ball that determines the position of the team. Each team has a ball of approximately four inches in diameter which is alternately kicked and chased by team members. The ball is rolled up onto a runner's bare toes and then flung forward (ouch!). Due to the rugged terrain, the ball frequently becomes wedged between rocks or in crevasses. To disengage the ball in these cases, the racers carry long, hand-carved, spoon-shaped sticks as they run. Occasionally the ball will be lost over the side of the cliff, so the elder continues to carve new balls all afternoon.

When enough runners have arrived (in this case there were 14 on each team) and the wagers have all been placed, the *cabeceros*, Ronrico and Desidero, gather the bets from their respective teams and go to face each other. The wagers may take the form of money or goods such as cloth, foodstuffs, or livestock. With great ceremony, the bets are presented and the *cabeceros* return to their respective teams.

After all the preparation, the actual start of the race is handled with surprisingly little fanfare. The teams walk slowly to an area that is not marked in any way but appears to have been designated as the start. Suddenly, the balls are in the air and the racers take off emitting chillingly primordial whoops and shouts.

Each team has a designated area alongside the race course similar to what we know as an aid station. The first item of business at each of these locations is the creation of a line of stones to represent the number of laps to be run. Stones are moved, one by one, to the side as the team completes a lap.

This particular race course is about three kilometers and the stones indicate that they expect to complete 34 laps. Tarahumara races are won when the first team completes the final lap, or when the last remaining member of the losing team drops out.

Felipe and team Medicine Man

Maro and team Medicine Man

Some of the women continue cooking. Others take their places beside the race course, holding out gourds containing *pinole* and water for the racers as they pass by. As the hours wear on, and the racers begin to tire, tacos made of tortillas and beans will be offered as well. The runners do not help themselves to any food or drink, and will take only what is handed directly to them.

The bright sun warms the afternoon as the race continues. Everyone takes an active interest. The hillside is dotted with spectators perched atop boulders scattered around the race course. Children play with smaller versions of wooden balls and sticks, in preparation for the day they too will be old enough to participate. Overhead, the vivid blue of the afternoon sky is interrupted by the jet stream of a plane enroute, perhaps, to Mexico City. It seems jarringly out of place, given the antediluvian nature of the events unfolding below.

Gradually the younger and older men begin to drop out, leaving only the most fit to continue the challenge. They have been running for several hours now, but the pace has slowed very little.

The elders' role grows in importance as tiring runners turn increasingly to them for encouragement, massage, new leather thongs, or whatever else may be needed. These "medicine men" seem, almost magically, to be able to produce a variety of requested items. In one case, a cigarette was plucked from the elder's headband for a needy runner. Unbelievably, the racers will occasionally take time out for a smoke break. However, as with many Native Americans, the smoking is more a ceremonial ritual than an addiction.

As the sun moves lower in the sky, the remaining runners are few. Runners have dropped out for reasons ranging from simple fatigue or muscle aches to, as was the case for the unfortunate Antonio, having been hit on the head by the wooden ball.

"It hurts and there's a pretty big bump," he admits when asked about his injury, "but I'll be alright, we're tougher than you white guys."

By dusk, there are three runners left on one team and only one on the other. As darkness looms, Ramon, the final runner on what will become the losing team, drops out. He has carried on a valiant struggle; but after kicking the ball all afternoon, he is losing the toenail on his big toe and is in a great deal of pain. This signals the end of the race.

Tarahumara Style Training

Victoriano Churro – First International Champion

The remaining three runners on the winning team thankfully stop running and head back to the house serving as their team headquarters. Of the 34 laps projected to be run, 32 have been completed over the course of the day. The balls are collected and given to the elder of the winning team who blesses them and saves them for a future race.

The proceeds from the betting are distributed among the happy winners and their families. In the glow of the sunset, runners, crew and spectators from winning and losing teams gather to rest, joke, laugh and eat. As night approaches, many roll up in blankets beside the fire and prepare to spend the night before undertaking the long journey home. The beat of a distant drum echoes through the night. The sound is strangely exciting, yet at the same time comforting.

Patrocinio comes over to sit by us. "It has been a good day," he says, as much to himself as to us, but we all hasten to agree, "Yes, it has." And we reflect upon our two divergent cultures, our victories and defeats, our lives and dreams, *kórima*. Perhaps we are not so very different after all.

Tarahumara Aid Station

THE LEGEND COMES TO LIFE

Patrocinio began to worry as he watched the roads being built closer and closer to his village. He pointed to a ridge not far away as he explained to Fisher, "They told us the roads would never cross that line, but I wonder who, besides us, will know or care if they do?"

Patrocinio believed that through their racing, the Tarahumara might serve as advocates for themselves and their traditional lifestyle. As a result, Fisher did what no previous sponsor had ever done. He analyzed the mistakes that were made in prior efforts and, with Patrocinio's help, began putting together a team of Tarahumara runners who would make yet another attempt at the world of international racing.

In addition to Patrocinio, who did not run but served as *cabecero* or team leader, the 1993 team included two members of the previous year's team, Antonio Palma, 28, and Felipe Torres, 22. Both very competent runners, they would also be able to provide valuable orientation for new members as they had the benefit of last year's experience with U.S.-style racing. Manuel Luna, 30, was recruited from a neighboring village. Although his village headman counseled against making the trip, Manuel agreed to go on the strength of his friend Antonio's assurances that he would be well-treated.

The remaining three runners came from the village of Panolachi. The two men who participated in the 1968 Olympics were from Panolachi and, perhaps as a result, racing has remained an important part of the culture despite the fact that roads have been built to the village. Cerrildo Chacarito, 38, Victoriano Churro, 55, and Churro's nephew, Benjamin Nava, 21, made up the Panolachi contingent.

For most, it was the first trip beyond the immediate vicinity of their villages. What courage it must have taken for these men to climb

into Fisher's Suburban and agree to be taken to an unfamiliar event in an unknown land! Passing through Cuidad Juarez, Benjamin's eyes widened at the sight of so many buildings and the traffic.

"I never knew there were so many cars, they look like a bunch of ants," he said.

If the cities they passed on their long journey were foreign, at least the mountainous terrain as they approached Leadville, Colorado was familiar.

"This used to be my Grandfather's farm," joked Antonio, a facetious reference to the amount of land that has been taken from them since the coming of the white man.

The Leadville Trail 100 is arguably the toughest race around. Beginning at over 10,000 feet of elevation, participants run over trails, ford rivers and cross mountain passes, including twice scaling 12,600-foot Hope Pass, to complete the 100 mile course in under 30 hours.

Aid stations offering food and drink are located at intervals along the route and a runner may have a crew to provide assistance with clothing and equipment needs. Pacers are allowed for the last 50 miles of the race. This is another individual who runs with the participant, keeping the runner on pace and providing emotional support. The pacer also serves a valuable safety function during the cold and dark night hours.

So why did Fisher pick this grueling race and why did the Tarahumara team agree to run it? Well, for several reasons. The first was simply a matter of timing. Falling as it does in the third week of August, the Leadville race is one of few that comes at a time when the men are not urgently needed at home for cultivation or harvest of their fields. Additionally, the Tarahumara, who traditionally run in similar conditions, considered the long distance and rough terrain to be to their advantage. Finally, a good showing in this race would demonstrate, beyond doubt, their superior abilities. As Frank Sinatra sings in the unrelated, but nevertheless apropos lyric, "If you can make it here, you can make it anywhere..."

Arriving in Leadville ten days before the race, preparation began in earnest. This year, the strategy would be different.

"These guys are professionals," said Fisher, "we're going to show them what to expect and provide the opportunity to experiment with both American and Tarahumara food, clothing and equipment and then we'll just sit back and let them run their race."

Ultrarunning, or running distances longer than a marathon, is growing in popularity in the United States. Aficionados are known as ultrarunners. Members of the ultrarunning community came together enthusiastically to serve as crew and pacers for the Tarahumara team. With their assistance, the Tarahumara had covered every foot of the course by race day and had the opportunity to try out equipment such as flashlights during a practice night run. In this way they avoided the problem that occurred the previous year when they ran with their lights pointed straight up, an obvious carry-over from running with torches

It was also during the night run that the team offered their crew a glimpse of their remarkable abilities. Having only been over this section of trail once before, this time they ran the still unmarked trail in the opposite direction, in the dark, at breakneck speed. Tom Sobel, himself a world-class athlete marveled at their talent.

"I was running with them," he said, "they never so much as hesitated when they came to a fork in the trail."

In spite of themselves, the crew frequently offered "helpful hints" to the Tarahumara team. Eventually this advice was met with a gentle roll of the eyes. "We know, we know," Antonio would reassure the concerned individual.

Although shoes had been provided, the team generally preferred their traditional *huaraches,* sandals made from tire tread and leather thong. In order to supply each runner with at least two pairs of *huaraches* for the race, a trip was made to the Leadville dump for tires.

Amazed that in the United States these tires are available for the taking, Felipe was thrilled with the quality. "In Mexico we would have to pay 50,000 pesos (about $17.00) for a tire," he said, "and then it would be bald. Look at how much tread is still on these!"

They worked hard for several days, making not only the *huaraches* needed for the race, but also cutting "blanks" of tread to take home for their families.

As the days remaining before the race dwindled, so did the level of activity. The team rested and ate large meals of tortillas, beans and corn to build their strength. On the afternoon of the day before the race, Fisher gathered the team and crew together for a "pep talk" and to go over last minute questions. Then Patrocinio took over, speaking at length in Tarahumara, he talked of teamwork and cooperation, he spoke of *kórima*. Then, forming everyone into a circle, each member of the team and crew went around the inside of the circle shaking hands and wishing the others luck.

The chilly early morning hours of August 21, 1993 saw a crowd of some 295 participants and their crews gathered in the streets of downtown Leadville in anticipation of the 4 a.m. start of the race. The Tarahumara aren't fond of crowds so they stayed near the back of the pack. When the gun signaled the start and runners moved out into the darkness, the Tarahumara team began the race in last place.

By the 40-mile point the leading Tarahumara runners, Victoriano and Cerrildo had moved up to 55th and 56th place. They were no where near the race leaders of course, but were running a very respectable race nonetheless. Crew members commented proudly among themselves and to others, "They're doing just as we suggested, taking it slow and running a conservative race."

From this point the race course began the steep ascent of Hope Pass, including a river crossing and some very rocky sections of trail...just the Tarahumara's cup of tea. By the turn around point at Winfield, 50 miles into the race, Victoriano had moved up to 20th place, with Cerrildo and Manuel right behind. What happened after that is hard to say because they were moving so fast that they beat their crew to the next aid station. Race officials at the 60-mile checkpoint, however, recorded Manuel as the leading member of the Tarahumara team and in fifth place overall. By this time the competitive aspect of the race for the Tarahumara team had become focused between their own villages, the *gringos* just happened to get passed in the process.

As the crew scrambled to get pacers in place for what had turned into a very serious race, the Tarahumara continued to gain on their competition. At the 72-mile point, Manuel was still leading the Tarahumara team and in second place overall. Victoriano and Cerrildo were just minutes behind. For the last 20 miles or so, the Tarahumara ingested only *pinole*, the cornmeal mixture that is a staple of their traditional diet.

Over rugged Sugarloaf Mountain, Victoriano passed Manuel to reclaim his place as the Tarahumara front-runner and, in doing so, also passed the race leader to move into first place overall.

Twenty hours, two minutes and thirty-three seconds after the race began, Victoriano Churro crossed the finish line to win the 1993 Leadville Trail 100. Cerrildo followed with a second place finish time of 20:43:06 and, despite problems with a broken *huarache* thong, Manuel managed a very respectable fifth place finish in 21:26:09.

The Tarahumara tribe is known for being able to run down a deer. They can't run faster, but they can run longer, until the animal drops from exhaustion. They ran this race in much the same way.

All the facts surrounding Victoriano's remarkable victory wouldn't surface until later. Registered as 38 years old, he told his pacer that he was actually 55 and a grandfather. The mystery was solved upon closer inspection of his immigration card. During the process he had been asked his year of birth and had replied "fifty-five." He meant he was 55 years old but instead his year of birth was erroneously recorded as 1955, which would have made him 38. And so Victoriano Churro, at age 55, became the oldest winner in the history of the race!

In the end, five of the six Tarahumara team members crossed the finish line, a notable accomplishment in a race where the overall completion rate is less than half. Only Felipe was unable to finish the race. He dropped out at 93 miles, suffering from a familiar runner's complaint, his new shoes, the *huaraches*, weren't broken in sufficiently before the race and had resulted in painful blood blisters.

The spectacular finishes of Victoriano, Cerrildo and Manuel had the crowd in a frenzy, but for those who followed the events closely, Antonio and Benjamin's finishes were no less remarkable. Antonio, who ran perhaps the most steady pace ever recorded, almost left his pacer behind when he actually sped up during the last 20 miles of the race. Benjamin struggled through the last few miles in agony to become, at age 21, the youngest finisher in the history of the race.

Kit Williams organizing the Tarahumara Team for the Leadville race

Unlike the other participants, many of whom prepared for months and even years, the Tarahumara didn't train specifically for this or any other race. They were able to run the way they did simply because their lifestyle enables them to maintain this level of fitness. The very simplicity of their running, even more distinguished by the surrounding world of high-tech shoes and special training diets, touched many hearts.

In stark contrast to the journey up from Mexico during which the prejudice against the Indians was so severe restaurant personnel were often hesitant to serve them, the Tarahumara would return to Chihuahua as heros. This time when they walk into the restaurant in Chihuahua, Mexican patrons and staff alike give them a standing ovation. Part of the strength of the Tarahumara is that they have always been a proud people, but in these men perhaps the pride is now a little more visible. Sometimes it even looks as though there might be a hint of a swagger to their step. They certainly earned it.

A small team of Tarahumara racers came to the 1993 Leadville Trail 100 and the result was *kórima* in its truest form. *Kórima* between the Tarahumara and their crew and pacers, between the Tarahumara and everyone who watched them run.

Note: Wilderness Expeditions would like to extend heartfelt thanks to all who have provided valuable assistance with crewing, pacing and financial support for this project.

Wilderness Expeditions requests your tax-deductible contribution to promote this project and offers special tours of the Copper Canyon for runners. The Tarahumara very much want to participate in international races where they and their traditions are respected. They need your assistance to travel to the U.S. and possibly beyond! It is now known that they have the talent, fitness and desire to be international ultra athletes, they just need the opportunity. Write for futher information:

Wilderness Research Expeditions
P.O. Box 86492 • Tucson, AZ 85754 • (520) 882-5341

Canyon Tarahumara – Semana Santa

Fiesta of the Virgin of Guadalupe

Mirrors flash in the moonlight as cloth ribbons sway to the beat of shoes stomping on the frozen winter earth. Fires dance while ghostly human figures are reflected on the stone and adobe mission walls. Women huddle under heavy blankets, keeping a silent vigil as their husbands and sons dance throughout the night.

The Tarahumara celebrate the *Fiesta of the Virgin of Guadalupe* on December 12, in honor of the Virgin Mary, Mother of God, who appeared to a humble Aztec, Juan Diego, in 1531. The Virgin Mary asked Juan Diego to build a temple where all the people of Mexico could receive her love and protection.

Although many Tarahumara are unaware of the story of the Virgin Mary, their celebration is not without rich tradition. The nocturnal festival is taken quite seriously, even though it is a time of merriment – dancing, drinking, and feasting.

Two lines of dancers file quietly into the mission. Prayers and supplications are given at the alter. Pairs of opposing matachines (dancers) advance and circle each other. They wear colorful costumes of the fiesta, each adorned with a corona (crown) – a wooden headdress covered with mirrors, cloth ribbons and other shiny objects, fastened with bandanas. Carrying a wand with ribbons dangling at the end, and a matraca (wooden whirl rattle), the matachines dance to Indian fiddles and guitars.

Dancing is the customary form of worship for the Tarahumara. Boys as young as ten years old are taught the matachine, with one or two youngsters often finding the stamina to dance all night.

The lines of matachines weave in and out, the hypnotic "clop, clop, clop" of the heeled shoes comes to an abrupt end as the mission bell rings and the dancers emit a high-pitched "whee-ho-ho." The dancers repeat their procession through the moonlit night into the dawn. (R.D.F., S.B.)

Prior to the festival, the Mountain Tarahumara erect 12 large arches of saplings and tree branches around the church grounds. Adorning the arches are *sereque*-sotol wreaths fashioned to resemble large flowers. Processions of dancing and drumming tribespeople follow the route marked by the arches, acting out the Via Dolorosa, or Way of the Cross, the Tarahumaras adaption of the incidents of Jesus' Passion.

Lacking trees, the Canyon Tarahumara instead place three crosses on the outskirts of the mission church.

Holy Thursday marks the first day of the fiesta, with the percussionist gathering participants with the beat of his drum. The congregation proceeds through the arches as a man plays the matraca (wooden whirl rattle). The matraca clears the Way of the Cross of harmful spirits, and signals the group to move on. The steady sound of drum beats, flute whistles, and violins lead the way. They are greeted in the plaza by the padre (priest) or gobernador.

At this time, groups of dancers are formed, the Fariseos (pharisees), the Soldados (soldiers), and the Pascoleros. The Fariseos and the Soldados become opposing "teams" which represent good and evil. Fariseos wear crude costumes, paint their bodies and use primitive instruments. Contrasting these dancers are the Soldados, who are more dignified than their counterparts and wear traditional costumes. These two groups participate in lighthearted wrestling matches symbolizing the clash between good and evil.

Traditionally dressed Tarahumara, as pictured in this section, are becoming increasingly rare and now inhabit only very isolated and remote areas. Most Tarahumaras throughout the sierras and barrancas have adopted western style attire. Influenced by modern pressures, the Tarahumara are losing their cultural identity. These changes come from an invasion of Mexican-mestizo settlers, and by well meaning but misguided missionaries and private citizens who give away used clothing by the truckload. **Please** *do not distribute cast offs of any type in these remote areas. For those wishing to help the Tarahumara, purchase traditional style cloth in Creel and distribute it in ten meter lengths.*

For others wishing to assist the Tarahumara, the publisher recommends purchasing traditional arts and crafts directly from the Indians or at the Tarahumara Mission Store in Creel. Further material assistance can be given to the Tarahumara Children's Hospital which has helped save the lives of thousands of these Native Americans.

Throughout the night, the sounds of drums beating are heard reverberating through the valleys and canyons. Huge bonfires dot the mountainside where family and friends gather to share stories, food, and tesqüino.

Good Friday's rituals are similar to Holy Thursday's, but with greater gaiety as the tesqüino drinking becomes hardier. The dancing continues, tesqüinadas (gatherings for eating and drinking) are held, and elections may take place at this time.

The final day of ceremonies is completed by wrestling matches between the Fariseos and Soldados. These awkward battles are are won when the opponent is thrown to the ground. The group that claims the most victories has the honor of "slaying" the effigy of Judas by setting fire to it. This marks the end of the Semana Santa celebration for the current year. If the participants pleased God with their performances, there will be much rain, good crops and a rich feast to look forward to next year.

Each ceremony, while rich in tradition, may differ markedly in detail and symbolism depending on the village's isolation, and the church and mestizo influences. (S.B.)

**Tarahumara Photography
by Luis G. Verplancken, S.J.**

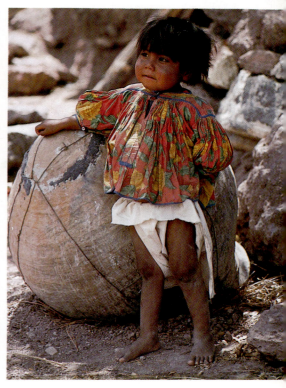

Estado de Chihuahua

La Gente y El Paisaje de Chihuahua

Un ilustre Maestro chihuahuense José Fuentes Mares realizó una disección de su tierra y sus habitantes que a continuación y con mucho respeto transcribo: -...Chihuahua es un paisaje desalmado y solo. Es una tierra sin agua, que hacia donde fina con Sonora y Sinaloa, se adueña de bosques y montañas en cabal equilibrio con el desierto...

Tierra exigüe que impone su carácter lo mismo al risco que al cauce de arroyos siempre secos; sin aguajes ni sombras, inclementes como los hielos y el sol.

Como los líquidos, los organismos y las almas se ajustan a su continente, proclaman sus virtudes y sus miserias...

Luego en el barbecho, el labriego sueña con la sombra y la lluvia. Hasta donde la santidad puede mundanizarse en la búsqueda del sustento, santo es quien un año y otro vuelve al surco, religión sin recompensa, dogmática sin paraíso...

Al lado de los pueblos se levantan también cuidades, hoy florecientes, en las que vale la vida no por lo que tiene de dádiva sino de conquista; ciudades sedientas y duras, cuñas de vida humana en la naturaleza bronca ...

Un 12 de octubre, en la confluencia de dos riachuelos, alguien dio el grito de ¡agua! Y se fundó Chihuahua...

El hombre de estos páramos es un navegante en la llanura ¡y como cala oírle mentar su vocación marinera en la tierra sin agua!:-¿Como esta usted don Pancho?

-Pos yo aquí, navegando....

Y sin embargo, nunca ha visto el mar, lo vieron sus abuelos, que adentraron la mar primero y luego la tierra sin dueño. Lo de hoy no es mas que el eco de la sangre castellana que sueña con el agua en el desierto...

En Chihuahua el mestizaje de razas fue limitadísimo. Criollos y españoles fueron los primeros colonizadores (no conquistadores) y criollos sus descendientes, fuertes como sus padres, frugales, rudos, independientes, buscadores de minas y criadores de rebaños en el siglo XVIII, cazadores de cabelleras indias en el siglo XIX. De ellos heredaron los hombres del llano y de la sierra sobre todo, profundo sentido de la dignidad personal y amor ilimitado a la libertad.

El hombre de Chihuahua nació abierto y liberal

Pocos -o nadie- se habrán preguntado por que en Chihuahua no hubo Guerra de Independencia. El aislamiento geográfico por un lado, el acendrado individualismo libertario por el otro, fueron factores de fuerza para que en estos lares funcionaran desde el primer momento gobiernos virtualmente autónomos y democráticos...

Hoy todo se encuentra muy cerca; en 1810 todo estaba muy lejos. El conflicto moral del Padre Hidalgo no cabía. Mis antepasados empezaron a abrir los ojos el día de su fusilamiento, y terminaron de abrirlos cuando la ciudad de México recibió jubilosa al Ejército de las Tres Garantías. Pasamos del Coloniato a la Independencia casi sin darnos cuenta de ello.

Pocos -o nadie- se habrán preguntado porque en Chihuahua tampoco hubo Guerra de Reforma. Esta guerra resultó incomprensible para los Chihuahuenses por la razón muy simple de ser todos liberales, hasta los curas.

Por ultimo obsérvese que Chihuahua fue uno de los focos principales, si no el más importante de la Revolución de 1910. Como en Coahuila, como en Sonora, en Chihuahua la Revolución no la hicieron peones sin tierras o caudillos hambrientos sino burgueses de clase media; Pascual Orozco, acomodado transportista de metales en la región serrana y Abraham González, tenedor de libros con estudios profesionales en alguna escuela norteamericana...

Entre la iniciativa de las sociedades abiertas y la inercia de las sociedades cerradas o igualitarias, el chihuahuense se inclinará siempre por la primera.

Asunto inagotable este del ser, hacer y que hacer del chihuahuense. Caminamos de prisa, desde sus orígenes vizcaínos fue una sociedad abierta, de iniciativas personales, sin afeites barrocos, nunca fue tierra fácil; el paraíso terrenal no estuvo por aquí, pero si así y todo el chihuahuense pudo desenvolverse, levantar ciudades, conseguir niveles de vida en otras partes insospechadas, es porque el hombre es un ser lleno de posibilidades en el trabajo y la libertad. Entender la vida como desafío es propio de mi gente. No desquite o bravuconería, sino desafío cargado de esperanza.

Por Chihuahua y los Alrededores. Rumbo al sur, a solo 9 kilómetros se encuentra SANTA EULALIA. Hacia 1702 unos mineros de Cusihuiriachi denunciaron unos ricos yacimientos de plata, rápidamente se pobló una región a la que se le llamó Santa Eulalia, sus minas fueron consideradas como las más ricas del mundo. Hoy la llamamos "cuna de la ciudad de Chihuahua". El pintoresco pueblito minero tiene además de sus caracteristicos callejones, en la entrada principal, un bello templo dedicado a Santa Eulalia de Mérida. Le recomendamos saborear la exquisita comida regional que se ofrece en modestos comedores y en el Restaurant El Mesón en donde los fines de semana se ameniza con música en vivo. No deje de visitar los miradores de Santo Domingo.

Meoqui/Delicias

DELICIAS es la ciudad más joven del estado, fue fundada en 1933. Su trazo urbano está basado en la rosa de los vientos, sus fundadores son conocidos como los Vencedores del Desierto. Visite los museos de Paleontología y de la Telefonía. El Hotel del Norte esta construido en los cascos de una antigua hacienda. Para comer pescado fresco le recomendamos los restaurantes que están al lado del camino a la cortina de la Presa de las Virgenes.

MEOQUI fue originalmente nombrado San Pablo, es una pequeña población colonial ubicada a 10 minutos al norte de Delicias, merece mención especial por su buen servicio, exquisita cocina y trato cordial, el Restaurant Tarahumara del Vado de Meoqui, después de comer le recomendamos visitar la plaza y la antigua iglesia de San Pedro y San Pablo. Celebran las fiestas patronales durante la última semana de Junio.

Rumbo al Noroeste por la carretera 16, a 48 kilómetros se localiza SANTA ISABEL, población utilizada por nuestros antepasados como punto de descanso cuando se viajaba en lomo de mula, era el sitio estratégico para pasar la noche, apacentar el ganado y las bestias de carga. Pancho Villa y sus Dorados descansaron alguna vez a la ribera del río Santa Isabel. Por la misma ruta, solo que a 104 kms. se encuentra CD. CUAUHTEMOC, población originalmente nombrada SAN ANTONIO DE LOS ARENALES, hoy está convertida en una pujante población gracias a los industriosos Menonitas, quienes debido a su religiosa dedicación al trabajo, han convertido las enormes praderas en fértiles tierras de labranza y fruticultura, no en vano están considerados como los mejores granjeros del mundo. Una visita a los Campos Menonitas le permitirá apreciar como se desarrollaba la vida a principios de siglo en una granja de la lejana Alemania. Saboree los embutidos y el famoso queso Menonita.

Rumbo al este de la ciudad de Chihuahua, a solo 28 kms., se localiza el Bosque de ALDAMA, entrando, al lado izquierdo, se aprecia una antigua capilla con cúpula, es la Misión de Santa Ana de Chinarras edificada en 1671 por, encargo del capitán Pedro Cano de los Ríos. Después de varios intentos de colonización, se inicio el poblado de la Villa de Aldama; hoy es una comunidad dedicada principalmente a las labores del campo. El Bosque de Aldama tradicionalmente ha sido visitado por los chihuahuenses en días de campo. Se le han adicionado modernos balnearios y restaurantes de comida típica. No deje de saborear la cajeta (ate) de membrillo que se elabora en esta población. Por la misma carretera a 144 kilómetros se encuentra COYAME, a lo largo del camino observará un bellísimo paisaje desértico; Coyame desde los tiempos más remotos ha sido conocido como un oasis. En un cerro ubicado a un kilómetro del caserío, se descubrieron unas hermosas grutas, que recientemente se iluminaron y acondicionó un acceso para ofrecerle seguridad al visitante, hoy no sólo los espeleólogos pueden gozar de esta belleza. En aproximadamente una hora usted podrá admirar lo que le tomó a la madre naturaleza construir millones de años. Hay además un balneario de aguas termales. Le sugerimos saborear la exquisita barbacoa de res que los lugareños sazonan con hierbas de la región.

CHIHUAHUA A TRAVES DEL TIEMPO

La Leal y Progresista ciudad de Chihuahua fue fundada el 12 de Octubre de 1709 con el nombre de San Francisco de Cuellar, posteriormente se convirtió en San Felipe el Real de Chihuahua. La población nace gracias a las riquísimas minas de Santa Eulalia, ubicadas a cuatro leguas, (9 kms) al este. Su fundación en el valle formado en la confluencia de los ríos Chuvíscar y Sacramento obedece a dos razones; la primera, las reales ordenanzas de 1573 que indicaban que las fundaciones de los nuevos asentamientos debían hacerse junto a los ríos; y la segunda, la necesidad de mayor cantidad de agua para el beneficio de los metales.

En estas enormes llanuras, se han forjado una clase peculiar de hombres y mujeres. La accidentada geografía seleccionó de manera natural los tipos. En el estado se empezaron a diversificar las actividades productivas; gracias a la bonanza de la minería floreció el comercio; asimismo, se inicio la ganadería, hoy por hoy una de las actividades económicas mas preponderantes en esta región. Solo los Apaches se interpusieron entre la prosperidad y el Chihuahuense.

Cuando en el centro y sur de nuestro país Hidalgo y los Insurgentes enarbolaban las nobles ideas independentistas, en esta lejana tierra se libraba una sangrienta guerra. Los Apaches eran más amenazantes que las diferencias que originaron el movimiento social por la Independencia. En 1880 en Tres Castillos se peleó la última de las batallas, en ella murió el legendario Jefe Apache Vitorio, fue derribado por dos tarahumaras -Mauricio Corredor y Roque-, lidereados por el General Joaquin Terrazas; a esta batalla solo sobrevivieron mujeres y niños, fue éste el principio del fin de esta tribu; posteriormente Gerónimo, el último líder Apache- se rindió al Ejercito Norteamericano.

En 1864 la ciudad de Chihuahua albergó al Presidente Don Benito Juárez y a su gabinete, convirtiéndose en sede de los poderes de la República. Juárez permaneció en territorio Chihuahuense durante la invasión francesa.

Cuando ascendió al poder el General Porfirio Díaz en 1877, ya la ciudad de Chihuahua contaba con 22 mil habitantes, en los almacenes de la ciudad se podían conseguir los más exquisitos productos europeos; esta población ya era el centro económico y político del estado.

En 1881 empezó la construcción del Palacio de Gobierno; el ferrocarril ya nos comunicaba a la ciudad de México, iniciándose en 1903 la construcción del ferrocarril Chihuahua al Pacífico. Por los rumbos de El Paseo Bolívar, la avenida Cuauhtémoc y la calle Juárez, se construyeron bellas mansiones con fachada de cantera. La ciudad reflejaba prosperidad. El Parque Lerdo y su hermosa arboleda era por donde las familias paseaban los domingos; desafortunadamente, aun faltaba por vivirse uno de los episodios más trágicos de la vida de la República, -la Revolución-, Los Dorados y su Comandante en Jefe el General Francisco Villa y sus Generales Pascual Orozco y Toribio Ortega entraron en escena. Después de diez años de sangrienta lucha y de la muerte de Carranza, Villa se retiró. Los que siguieron fueron años muy difíciles hasta que por 1940 inició la recuperación y estabilidad política. En 1954 se fundó la Universidad Autónoma de Chihuahua y a partir de entonces, empezó la era moderna de la ciudad.

Atractivos Turisticos de la Ciudad de Chihuahua

Gracias también a los ricos yacimientos argentíferos de Santa Eulalia, en 1727 se inició la edificación de una de las más bellas iglesias del norte de México, la CATEDRAL DE CHIHUAHUA, los mineros accedieron a donar un real por cada marco de plata con la idea de construir un templo digno, enorme, sin igual en la comarca. La Catedral es un enorme edificio de tres naves con una amplísima portada; en 1772 hubo una grave crisis provocada por los Apaches y los Comanches, por lo que los fondos de la obra tuvieron que aplicarse a los gastos de guerra. Debido a esto y al factor de un período de baja en la producción de plata, la obra tardó en concluirse casi cien años. Su fachada estilo churrigueresco -labrada por las expertas manos de los canteros locales- es una verdadera belleza, en su interior sobresalen los altares mayores, el original de cantera labrada, y el que construyó en 1929 en mármol el maestro Luigi Tomassi. De méritos para mención aparte son: el Cristo Negro de Mapimi, el enorme órgano y los candiles de cristal veneciano. MUSEO DE ARTE SACRO, se ubica en los sótanos de la Catedral; se exhiben lienzos de temas biblicos que datan del siglo XVII atribuidos a los maestros Alzíbar y Cabrera, fundadores de la prestigiada Academia de San Carlos. Se conserva la silla -tapizada con el escudo de El Vaticano- y otros objetos que utilizó en 1990 S.S. el Papa Juan Pablo II durante su visita a Chihuahua. En la plaza de Armas, en la explanada del frente de catedral, se ubica la estatua del fundador de la ciudad Don Antonio Deza y Ulloa. Calle de por medio, se encuentra un edificio que data de 1721, -se construyó para dar cabida a las Casas Reales-, es el PALACIO MUNICIPAL, en 1770 se le agregaron unos portales de cantera en donde estuvo el primer mercado ambulante de Chihuahua. En 1906 se le encargó al prestigiado arquitecto Julio Corredor Latorre que modificara la construcción original ya que en 1866 el edificio había sido fragmentado y vendido en partes para obtener fondos para la guerra contra los franceses. En 1988 se reintegró al municipio la propiedad original. En la parte sureste de la ciudad, aun se puede admirar un buen tramo de una obra de arcos de cantera, le conocemos como el ACUEDUCTO COLONIAL, fue construido bajo la dirección de los Jesuitas a mediados del siglo XVIII, solucionó el enorme problema de proveer a la creciente población del vital líquido y a la vez ayudó a embellecer la villa, ya que el agua del rio Chuvíscar, llegaba a una fuente a la plaza, derramando sus excedentes sobre árboles y flores.

En 1811, Don Miguel Hidalgo y Costilla y los Insurgentes que lo acompañaban fueron capturados por los soldados del Rey en Acatita del Bajan, hoy estado de Coahuila, se les trajo a esta ciudad, en donde se les mantuvo prisioneros. A Hidalgo, se le despojó de su condición clerical; todos fueron juzgados y sentenciados a muerte. El cura fue fusilado a espaldas de la Iglesia del Colegio de Nuestra Señora de Loreto (hoy Palacio de Gobierno), el 30 de Julio de 1811. Honramos el sitio exacto de su ejecución con un ALTAR A LA PATRIA. Calle de por medio está el PALACIO FEDERAL, se conserva la torre y el calabozo donde estuvo prisionero el Padre de la Patria, fue convertido en el MUSEO CALABOZO DE HIDALGO; ahí se exhiben copias de importantes documentos del movimiento independentista. PALACIO DE GOBIERNO edificado en 1881 originalmente en dos pisos, fue consumido en 1941 por el fuego, durante el cual, desafortunadamente, se consumió el archivo histórico. Al ser reedificado, se le agregó un piso más; alberga al Honorable Congreso del Estado, las oficinas del Gobernador y varias oficinas gubernamentales, entre ellas una dedicada a proporcionar información turística. En las paredes de la planta baja, Don Aaron Piña Mora realizó unos murales en donde se ilustra la historia de la región a partir de que el primer hombre europeo pisó estas tierras. Frente a la entrada principal del palacio de gobierno esta la PLAZA HIDALGO, con un monumento en el centro que honra a los héroes del movimiento de la Independencia. IGLESIA DE SAN FRANCISCO, sitio en donde estuvo sepultado el cuerpo decapitado del Padre de la Patria antes de que sus restos fueran trasladados al Angel de la Independencia en la ciudad de México. Además es apreciado por ser una de las escasas muestras de arquitectura colonial en nuestra ciudad. De gran valor didáctico es considerado el MUSEO DE LA LEALTAD REPUBLICANA "CASA DE JUAREZ", este edificio fue Palacio Nacional, albergó al presidente Don Benito Juárez y a su gabinete durante la época de la invasión francesa, se exhiben manuscritos del Benemérito de las Américas y mobiliario de la época. CENTRO DE ARTE CONTEMPORANEO, importante muestra de arte, acopio de piezas de artistas mexicanos con salas especiales para chihuahuenses de reconocida fama internacional como Siqueiros, Sebastián y Domínguez entre otros. CENTRO CULTURAL CHIHUAHUA, hermoso edificio de cantera, reflejo del esplendor de la vida de los hacendados a principios de siglo; perteneció a Don Luis Terrazas (1829-1923), prominente ganadero y hombre de negocios. Fue inclusive gobernador de Chihuahua. Hoy alberga salas de conferencias, conciertos y una muestra de vasijas de la cultura Paquimé. CENTRO CULTURAL UNIVERSITARIO "QUINTA GAMEROS" magnífica mansión considerada como una de las más bellas muestras del eclectisismo francés no solo de México sino de América Latina. Fue edificada por el colombiano Julio Corredor Latorre a principios de siglo. Inmejorable escenario para mostrar la colección de muebles estilo Art Noveau propiedad de la familia Requena, así como exposiciones itinerantes. Sus vitrales, escaleras y candiles, son dignos · de mención. MUSEO DE LA REVOLUCION MEXICANA, también conocido como la "QUINTA LUZ" casa que habitó hasta su muerte doña Luz Corral de Villa, viuda del controvertido General Francisco Villa. Se exhibe el automóvil que manejaba el Caudillo el 20 de Julio de 1923 cuando fue emboscado en Hidalgo del Parral, así como documentos, fotografías y armas de la época. MAUSOLEO DE VILLA, cripta que él mismo mandó construir en lo que era el panteón "De La Regla", actualmente es el Parque Revolución; solo que nunca la pudo utilizar debido a que a su muerte, primero se le sepultó en Hidalgo del Parral y posteriormente sus restos

fueron trasladados a la Cd. de México en donde finalmente descansa en el Monumento de la Revolución. CASA CHIHUAHUA SIGLO XIX, recinto dedicado a exposiciones de arte, conciertos y exhibiciones de artesanías. MUSEO COMUNITARIO TARIKE dedicado básicamente a la historia regional. Hace más de dos siglos, una devota dama en su testamento, mandó construir el Templo de SANTA RITA, patrona de la ciudad. PUERTA DE CHIHUAHUA esta colosal escultura ubicada a la entrada sur de la ciudad se debe al genio de SEBASTIAN, uno de los hijos más notables de Chihuahua.

Paso del Norte: Hoy Ciudad Juárez

La fronteriza Ciudad Juárez se encuentra localizada en un extenso valle a orillas del río Bravo frente a su vecina la ciudad de El Paso, Tx. Situada al norte de la ciudad de Chihuahua, tiene una altitud de 1144 msnm., clima árido y extremoso, combina lo antiguo y lo moderno con amable espíritu provinciano y un progreso económico por encima de la media nacional; es uno de los centros maquiladores más importantes del País, una ciudad dinámica que al mismo tiempo ofrece centros de diversión, paisajes urbanos, artesanías y construcciones antiguas que hablan de su historia.

Desde tiempos inmemoriales, y aún a la llegada de los españoles fueron grupos indígenas seminómadas conocidos hoy como los Sumas, Mansos y Jumanos quienes ocuparon la región donde actualmente se encuentra esta ciudad. Los nativos se dedicaban a la caza, agricultura, pesca y recolección. La cultura que desarrollaron estos grupos se adaptó maravillosamente a la geografía hostil de la región permitiéndoles permanecer aquí durante muchos años.

La llegada de los españoles a estas tierras ocasionó cambios tan profundos que propiciaron la asimilación total de los nativos. Se cree que los primeros europeos con los que tuvieron contacto fueron Alvar Nuñez Cabeza de Vaca, Andres Dorantes, Alonzo del Castillo y el negro Estebanico, quienes luego de un largo peregrinar cruzaron el río Bravo hacia 1532, dirigiéndose a la costa del pacífico.

En 1539 fray Marcos de Niza salió de la ciudad de México en busca de la mística Cíbola, una de las 7 ciudades de oro. Al año siguiente motivado por las buenas noticias de Niza, partió la celebre expedición de Francisco Vázquez de Coronado, quienes exploraron parte de la actual región de Ciudad Juárez, avanzando mucho mas al norte. Esta expedición fracasó en su principal objetivo; el encontrar las 7 ciudades de oro.

La primer noticia documentada sobre la llegada de los europeos a lo que actualmente ocupa esta ciudad la tenemos en la entrada que hicieron los frailes Agustín Rodríguez, Francisco López y Juan de Santa María, quienes autorizados por el Virrey y acompañados de una escolta de soldados exploraron el río Conchos hasta su desembocadura en el río Bravo; continuaron aguas arriba por el Bravo llegando al paraje donde estaría el Paso del Norte y continuaron junto al río hasta alcanzar el territorio conocido hoy de los indios pueblo, bautizándolo con el nombre de San Felipe de Nuevo México. Desafortunadamente los misioneros encontraron la muerte en manos de los nativos.

No fue sino hasta fines del Siglo XVI, con la entrada de Juan de Oñate al Nuevo México que se efectuó una nueva incursión a la región que nos ocupa. Después de cruzar el río Conchos, Oñate alcanzó los médanos de Samalayuca y mas adelante, el 20 de abril 1598, localizó lo que sería el sitio mas adecuado para cruzar el río Bravo, que en lo sucesivo se conocería como Paso del Norte.

Junto con Oñate llegaron los Franciscanos quienes empezaron a evangelizar a los nativos, contribuyendo con esto a que el 8 de Diciembre de 1659 Fray García de San Francisco fundara la Misión de Nuestra Señora de Guadalupe de los Mansos del Paso del Norte dándose el inicio de la actual Cd. Juárez.

De 1680 a 1693 fue refugio de la provincia del Nuevo México, al recibir a Don Antonio de Otermín quien asediado por las hordas barbaras capitaneadas por el gobernadorcillo "Pope", tuvo la necesidad de venir a refugiarse a esta incipiente localidad incluida dentro de la jurisdicción de la Nueva Vizcaya. Consecuentemente en este lapso, fue asiento de la provincia d el Nuevo México sirviendo de gran utilidad ya que con el raquítico reten de soldados que traían, logró el que se elevase a la categoría de "Presidio", al que se le denominó "Presidio de Nuestra Señora del Pilar del río del Paso del Norte".

En 1824, al haber quedado formado el primer Congreso Constituyente del Estado de Chihuahua, el 24 de mayo cambió su categoría asignándosele el nombre de "Pueblo Paso del Norte".

En 1865 el 4 de Agosto, llegó a la Villa Paso del Norte, el entonces presidente de la República Lic. Benito Juárez y su gabinete, sirviendo de albergue al representante de la patria. Permanecieron hasta el 13 de Noviembre, para regresarse a la Cd. de Chihuahua y volver nuevamente el 18 de Diciembre para no partir hasta el 18 de junio de 1866. Estando en la localidad, dictó benéficos acuerdos para la zona entre los que destaca la delimitación de los "partidos" predios que a la fecha prevalecen.

Tanto la presencia de Don Antonio de Otermín como la de Don Benito Juárez, dieron la consistencia necesaria para que el Escudo de nuestra ciudad ostente al axioma "Refugio de la Libertad", aplicable por la estancia de Don Antonio de Otermin y "Custodio de la República" adjudicándose este último a la presencia del "Benemérito de las Américas".

Tomando en consideración la relevante actitud del benemérito, por Decreto del Congreso del Estado de Chihuahua, promulgado el 24 de julio de 1888 y publicado el 30 del mismo mes, el nombre de "Villa Paso del Norte" cambia por el de Ciudad Juárez, ordenamiento que entró en vigor el 16 de septiembre de 1888.

Cuidad Juárez y sus Alrededores
Medanos de Samalayuca

Aproximadamente a 51 kilómetros al sur de Cd. Juárez por la carretera Panamericana se encuentran los Medanos de Samalayuca, hermosa zona de arenas blancas. Notable tanto por su extensión, como por los fósiles marinos que se encuentran en el área, testimonio de la existencia de un mar en épocas remotas. Lo más admirable de esta zona es la movilidad de las dunas; cuando sopla el viento, eleva cortinas de una finísima arena blanca que a la luz del sol se torna dorada, propiciando todo un espectáculo natural y haciendo a la vez que las colinas cambien de lugar. Bajo las arenas se encontraron vestigios de casas habitación, artefactos rústicos fabricados en hueso y piedra, así como fósiles de mamíferos terrestres. Otra peculiaridad del lugar es que existe gran diversidad de flora y fauna.

El vocablo Samalayuca es sorprendentemente de origen Náhuatl, así lo conocieron los primeros colonizadores que pasaron por la comarca hace mas de cuatrocientos años, por lo que se puede deducir que por aquí pasaron las tribus Nahuas cuando se dirigían al sur en su peregrinar en busca de la tierra prometida.

Aquí existe un vasto patrimonio cultural de gran ayuda para el entendimiento de la historia representado por medio del arte rupestre con más de tres mil petrograbados en varios conjuntos donde destacan figuras femeninas, animales, escenas rituales, escenas de cacería, y numerosas construcciones de signos entrelazados. Abundan también temas místicos y rituales así como instrumentos que fueron utilizados por los grupos que habitaron la zona, evidenciando su grado de desarrollo social y cultural.

Villa Ahumada

Fue fundada en el año de 1874, con el nombre de "Labor de la Magdalena". Es el municipio más grande del estado con más de 17 mil km2. Se localiza a 130 kilómetros de Ciudad Juárez y a 247 kilómetros de la ciudad de Chihuahua. Su altitud sobre el nivel del mar es de 1205 metros. El clima es extremoso con una temperatura máxima de 43 grados centígrados y una mínima de - 10 grados.

Cuenta con 127 localidades entre las que destacan Villa Ahumada como cabecera municipal, El Carrizal, Moctezuma y San Lorencito, entre otras. Tiene más de 13,000 habitantes y su principal actividad es la agricultura, seguida por la industria y servicios. Dentro del área se localizan varios puntos de interés como: La Misión de San Fernando construida en el siglo XVII, ubicada en el poblado de El Carrizal y la capilla de Santa Gertrudis, construida en el siglo XIX a un costado de la Misión de San Fernando. Asimismo, el edificio de la estación de ferrocarril construido a principios de siglo durante la Revolución por ordenes del General Francisco Villa, hoy convertido en museo.

Valle de Juárez

Esta región esta formada por varios poblados pertenecientes al municipio y que tienen como peculiaridad la vecindad con el Río Bravo. Destacan el poblado de Zaragoza, El Sauzal, San Agustín, San Isidro y Jesús Carranza entre otros. Todos ellos localizados en una extensión aproximada de 100 km. Entre los principales atractivos en esta zona sobresalen:

Museo de San Agustín

Está ubicado en el kilómetro 29 de la Carretera Juárez-Porvenir en el Valle de Juárez. Es un pequeño museo que en su interior muestra exposiciones permanentes de cartografía antigua, fotos de Ciudad Juárez, filminas, pueblos viejos y paleontología. Se exhiben piezas como fósiles de mamut, molares, colmillos y mandíbulas de aproximadamente 400 millones de años. (Era cuaternaria). Restos de utilería en piedra, metales, mortero y eulitos, representativos de los nativos que habitaron esta región.

Otro sitio de importancia son

Los arenales "La Colorada" ubicado entre San Agustín y Jesús Carranza, lugar ideal para pasear con la familia de día de campo. Existen algunos otros lugares que se prestan para paseos dominicales a lo largo de la carretera No. 2 que recorre todo el Valle de Juárez; la mayoría de ellos cuentan con albercas, restaurantes y otros servicios.

Misión de Nuestra Señora de Guadalupe del Paso del Norte

El prestigio personal de los misioneros y el progreso en la agricultura y la ganadería hizo que los indígenas aceptaran la apertura de una Iglesia en el territorio de los mansos y sumas en el lugar conocido como Paso del Norte. En 1659 Fray García de San Francisco de Zúñiga siendo custodio de la Misión de Senecú (actualmente al sur de Albuquerque Nuevo México), recibió una comisión de indios mansos y sumas que le solicitaran el establecimiento de una misión para hacerse cristianos.

El 8 de Diciembre de 1659 Fray García de San Francisco acompañado de Fray Juan de Salazar y diez familias de indios cristianos de Senecú, construyeron un oratorio provisional con ramas y lodo y un monasterio techado con paja. El 5 de Enero de 1668 se inauguró la nueva iglesia de la Misión de Nuestra señora de Guadalupe. Ese día se bautizaron 100 indios. Fray García de San Francisco residió por l2 años en la Misión de Guadalupe y volvió a la misión de Senecú, donde murió. Los Franciscanos duraron 139 años en la Misión desde 1659 hasta 1798.

La Misión de Guadalupe no es solo una muestra de la cultura barroca; es un monumento de fe, arte y belleza. Es el único ejemplar que sobrevivió en su totalidad a la destrucción general acaecida con motivo del levantamiento indígena del año de 1680.

Los elementos que sobresalen de este edificio son los siguientes: la construcción es de adobe con entrada principal y dos puertas laterales; pórtico sencillo y ojo de buey de mampostería, todo ello recientemente restaurado siguiendo el trazado de un grabado antiguo. El techo destaca por su calidad artística, asimismo el hecho de que como los misioneros vinieron de la Península Ibérica, donde imperó la influencia árabe; fue plasmada en los artesonados civiles y religiosos que ellos mismos diseñaron y construyeron. Asimismo, en La Misión de Guadalupe se hacen presentes elementos indígenas como son las decoraciones rectangulares, el trenzado, las estrellas circulares, los perfiles denteados y las paletas serpenteadas. El centro de la Iglesia cuenta con un altar de piedra de sillería colocado durante la ultima restauración del Santuario donde yacen los restos de los primeros pobladores. El suelo es de piedra Malpaís. Existe un coro de madera en la parte posterior de la iglesia sostenido en dos elegantes columnas de madera labrada coronadas de un capitel ancho. En la cabecera del presbiterio se encuentra un retablo central con la imagen de La Virgen de Guadalupe en una hornacina de cristal y madera finamente labrada. El conjunto es barroco de mano mexicana del siglo XVIII con inclusión de elementos indígenas.

Después de la fundación de la Misión de Guadalupe se construyó la MISIÓN DE SAN JOSÉ, está ubicada en la Calle Francisco Márquez y Reforma en la Col. San José, su permanencia data de los años de 1785-86, sirviendo además por mucho tiempo como puesto de vigía para detectar la proximidad de las ordas bárbaras que incursionaban frecuentemente en la población.

San José fue edificado por órdenes del visitador de provincia José de Galvez, comisionando para la construcción al comandante Pedro José de la Fuente, quién localizó un punto ubicado en un lugar estratégico en la parte suroeste de la localidad denominado fuerte de los indios. Los lugareños lo denominaban como el "Pueblito" y por un lapso de casi cien años se mantuvo en abandono, ya que se localizaba a 6 km de distancia de los núcleos de la población y llegar a este lugar no era fácil debido a que no se contaba con los caminos apropiados.

Por este lugar hizo su entrada Don Benito Juárez. Desde los años 1865-66 fueron delineadas sus calles iniciándose con este trazo el recorrido hacia el centro de la ciudad llamándolo Camino Nacional. En la parte posterior se encuentra un panteón que data de entre 1850 y 1870. Contiene monumentos de cantera con expresión estilística semejantes a los del Santuario de Guadalupe en la ciudad de Chihuahua. En 1910 era propiedad de Don Calixto Azcárate quién lo vendió a Don Inocente Ochoa cuyos restos descansan en este sitio.

SANTUARIO DE SAN LORENZO - Uno de los templos más hermosos ·de esta ciudad es este templo cuya construcción data de finales del siglo XVII. Fue destruido entre 1828-29 por una enorme crecida del cauce del Río Bravo, en 1831 fue reconstruido y a la fecha se le han hecho algunas otras modificaciones. Enfrente de la iglesia se encuentra la Plaza de San Lorenzo. Esta iglesia se localiza en la Av. Valle de Juárez y Fray Junípero Sierra.

Museos en Cd. Juárez

La ciudad cuenta con interesantes sitios históricos y culturales como son: Museo Histórico también conocido como el Museo de la Ex-aduana es uno de los más antiguos, construido a finales del siglo XIX e inaugurado el 10 se Septiembre de 1889, es de estilo francés y fue ocupado durante muchos años por la Aduana Fronteriza, fue sede de uno de los acontecimientos de más trascendencia en la Historia de México.

El edificio que alberga hoy el museo histórico nació ante la necesidad administrativa de control fiscal, es una edificación que tiene otros locales; destaca la Garita de Metales que se encuentra en la esquina de Francisco Villa y Vicente Guerrero.

En Octubre de 1909, -en este sitio tuvo lugar la entrevista entre Porfirio Diaz y William H. Taff. La aduana fronteriza cambió su hosco aspecto por aparente lujo teniendo como elementos decorativos pilastras, candiles y cortinajes. Espectacular fue el derroche de lujo de esta entrevista entre los presidentes de Estados Unidos y México para tratar el litigio creado por las desviaciones del Río Bravo obteniendo hasta 1967 que se regresara a México el territorio hoy conocido como El Chamizal. La aduana fronteriza fue sede de la firma del "Convenio de Ciudad Juárez" representando a las fuerzas de la revolución Don Francisco I. Madero y José María Pino Suárez, y por parte del gobierno porfirista Francisco S. de Carbajal. El 17 de Mayo de 1911 se acordó la suspensión de las actividades bélicas en todo el territorio nacional con el compromiso de la renuncia del General Porfirio Díaz a la Presidencia de la República. Durante la primera mitad del siglo XX, la aduana tuvo poco que administrar y fiscalizar debido a la baja del comercio y la industria; fue hasta 1948 y 1954 que se reestableció debido a un mayor auge en la frontera.

Estado para el efecto de destinarlo al establecimiento de un museo histórico, abriendo sus puertas el 18 de Julio de 1990.

Cuenta con 10 salas con exposiciones permanentes que representan una semblanza de la historia de México abarcando desde las culturas que florecieron en nuestro país antes de la llegada de los españoles, para dar paso a la conquista, Virreinato e Independencia. Una sala está destinada a la cultura Paquimé; le sigue la sala del comercio, de las épocas de la Reforma, el Porfiriato y finalmente 2 salas dedicadas a la Revolución Mexicana. Otro de los sitios no menos importante es el Museo de Arqueología, se encuentra situado en el interior del Parque Nacional Chamizal; muestra una gran cantidad de réplicas de las piezas originales de]as culturas del sur del país. En él podemos apreciar la época prehispánica y en general la historia de México. En la planeación y museografía colaboró el poeta tabasqueño Carlos Pellicer. Se pretendía hacer sentir no solo la sensibilidad artística de los hombres mesoamericanos, sino la monumentalidad de sus obras esculpidas. Las réplicas de relevantes ejemplos escultóricos constituyen colección única en el mundo.

Entre los trabajos y replicas relevantes se encuentran: del arte olmeca una cabeza colosal; de los teotihuacanos, toltecas y aztecas que habitaron en el altiplano central destacan los mascarones de Tláloc y Quetzalcóatl, atlantes y guerreros y la enigmática Coatlicue; no podían faltar ejemplos del arte Maya, de los Mixtecos, Zapotecos, Huastecos y Tarascos.

La fachada principal es de tipo contemporáneo con muros de ladrillo, losa y concreto.

Cuenta con tres salas para exposiciones itinerantes generalmente de escultura, pintura y grabado; ofrece además interesante colección de fósiles encontrados en la región; asimismo en sus jardines se exhiben reproducciones de piezas pertenecientes a las diferentes culturas del País. También tiene una sala de conferencias donde se destacan las actividades más sobresalientes de la época prehispánica.

El Museo de Arte e Historia fue puesto en funcionamiento por el Programa Nacional Fronterizo el 7 de Marzo de 1964 por el Arq. Pedro Ramírez Vázquez; la museografía se planeó cuidadosamente a base de fotomurales, maquetas, obras originales, copias en fibra de vidrio y otros materiales de las obras más representativas de las artes plásticas del arte Mexicano que se extiende desde el preclásico hasta el siglo XX. Los objetos artesanales y las artes gráficas de datos estadísticos forman parte del acervo que a propios y extraños le ayudaran a entender más a México. Desde 1970 la preocupación de los directivos del Museo fue conseguir en forma temporal, obras de los más altos valores nacionales sin perder de vista a los artistas locales y de la región. Se han expuesto trabajos de hombres que han traspasando los límites marcados por la frontera norte del país como Posadas, Orozco y Hurd.

Los juarenses gozan además de un recinto donde se ofrecen conferencias y obras de teatro, conformando un ambiente cultural y que ya existía aunque aislado. Poco a poco las actividades del museo han ido cambiando conforme al interés de la población por lo que recientemente se le agregó una sala para espectáculos permitiendo así la ampliación de sus planes hacia la escena. La colección permanente de obras donadas por artistas sobresalientes se inició con el "Nacimiento de Tauro" que José García Ocejo obsequiara en 1966, a partir de esa fecha se ha aumentado notablemente contando en la actualidad con cerca de 40 obras.

La **GALERIA QUINTA ANITA** Situada en una hermosa mansión de la familia Bermudez, ubicada en 16 de Septiembre y Uruguay, se fundó con el hecho de promover los productos artísticos y artesanales de diferentes Estados de la República, para autofinanciar programas de asistencia social. Cuenta además con un interesante Museo alusivo a Francisco Villa y la época de la Revolución Mexicana.

GARITA DE METALES construida en 1889 sirvió en su época para el control de los metales que eran transportados por esta zona.

ANTIGUA PRESIDENCIA MUNICIPAL Fue construida en 1947, está ubicada en la Av. Mariscal entre las avenidas 16 de Septiembre y Vicente Guerrero ahí se encuentra un mural que explica la historia de la región desde la fundación de Ciudad Juárez hasta los tiempos modernos.

CENTRO ARTESANAL Contiene las multicolores manifestaciones artesanales de toda la República, ahí se consiguen también los productos más representativos de cada Estado.

CENTROS NOCTURNOS Existe gran variedad de lugares de diversión nocturna; desde un romántico bar hasta fabulosas discotecas que le permitirán demostrar sus habilidades para el baile.

MONUMENTO A DON BENITO JUAREZ Es el monumento de mayor importancia en la ciudad. Se encuentra localizado en la calle Vicente Guerrero entre Ramón Corona y Constitución en la zona centro. Es una obra arquitectónica que se realizó por iniciativa del entonces gobernador del Estado Don Enrique C. Creel, con motivo de las fiestas conmemorativas que iban a realizarse en la ciudad de México. En 1909 el entonces presidente de la República General Porfirio Díaz estuvo presente en esta ciudad en la ceremonia en donde se colocó la primera piedra, la obra se terminó un año mas tarde, inaugurándose el 16 de Septiembre de 1910.

PARQUE CENTRAL HERMANOS ESCOBAR Fue inaugurado el 10 de Octubre de 1997 ofrece espacio para realizar actividades recreativas como, paseos en lancha en el lago artificial, juegos mecánicos; instalaciones deportivas, y áreas verdes, es un lugar ideal para fomentar el deporte y sobre todo la convivencia familiar.

PARQUE CHAMIZAL Se localiza por la entrada del Puente Internacional de Córdova. Este es un sitio muy importante en la historia de la ciudad ya que debido a la desviación que a lo largo de los tiempos sufrió el río Bravo, éstos terrenos estaban en posesión de los Estados Unidos de Norteamérica. México inició un litigio que afortunadamente concluyó amistosamente y en 1967 estos terrenos fueron regresados a nuestra nación, convirtiéndolos en un Parque que permite practicar varias actividades de recreación.

Circuito Arqueologico Casas Grandes · Madera

I. Circuito Arqueologico

En el noroeste del estado de Chihuahua nos encontramos en la region arqueológica más importante del noreste de México. Los vestigios de una gran civilización establecida desde el valle de Casas Grandes hasta las faldas de la Sierra Madre en Madera, son como una ventana al pasado, donde la Cultura Mogollón manifestó hace más de novecientos años, la magia de su arquitectura e ingeniería hidráulica, reflejadas tanto en la gran urbe de Paquimé como en las impresionantes construcciones en acantilados y cavidades naturales como es el caso de Cuarenta Casas y la Cueva Grande por mencionar algunos.

El recorrido que ahora presentamos nos permite conocer las maravillas que nos han heredado nuestros antecesores en el norte de México, mismas que hoy en día muestra el alto grado de desarrollo qua existía antes de la llegada de españoles, así como los contrastantes sucesos históricos que a través del tiempo se han manifestado en esta porción de territorio del estado más grande la República Mexicana. Lo invitamos a compartir con nosotros estos fascinantes recorridos que indudablemente será un viaje extraordinario para disfrutarlo en compañía de sus familiares y amigos.

II. Su Arqueologia

Sin duda alguna la República Mexicana ofrece una increíble variedad de sitios arqueológicos desarrollados a lo largo de todo el país. En la actualidad las investigaciones demuestran una clara definición entre lo que fue el centro y sur del país conocido como Mesoamérica y lo que fue su frontera norte conocida como la gran Chichimeca.

En la región mesoamericana los desarrollos culturales fueron similares, existiendo un proceso bastante homogéneo que inicia hacia el año 2000 A.C. con el establecimiento de aldeas agrícolas sedentarias que con el tiempo llegaron a desarrollar civilizaciones y estados.

La frontera Norte de Mesoamérica nunca fue estable ni similar en su desarrollo cultural, ya que en ella habitaron diversos grupos nómadas y sedentarios que se tuvieron que adaptar a una región, en la que las condiciones de vida eran más adversas debido en gran parte a su territorio desértico y su clima extremoso sobre todo durante el invierno. Los primeros pobladores de esta región arribaron probablemente hace más de 1,000 años, sin embargo la evidencia arqueológica nos muestra fechas de 6,000 años A.C. Estos pobladores habitaron en abrigos rocosos, aprovechando las formaciones naturales. A medida que fueron implementando las técnicas agrícolas fueron ocupando las márgenes de los ríos. Estos primeros agricultores sembraron plantas originarias de Mesoamérica como el maíz, frijol, calabaza y algodón, adaptándolos a las diferentes condiciones climáticas con base en técnicas cada vez más complejas, que permitieron mayor sedentarismo. Las primeras aldeas fueron casas pequeñas generalmente de planta circular u ovalada y piso excavado a diferente profundidad. Estas construcciones fueron conocidas como casas-foso, su techo era de varas y adobe en forma de domo con una entrada lateral.

Explorando un Mundo Olvidado - Carlos Lazcano Sahagún

Hace aproximadamente 2000 años inició su desarrollo una de las culturas indias más fascinantes y desconocidas de Norteamérica: la cultura Paquimé. Esta cultura tuvo su origen en los grupos mogollón que se fueron extendiendo desde el sur oeste de lo que actualmente son los Estados Unidos hasta el noroeste de México. A partir del año 700 los mogollones que se habían instalado en el Valle de Casas Grandes, Chihuahua, empezaron a evolucionar de una manera distinta, llegando a conformar, con el tiempo, a la cultura Paquimé, la cual tuvo su máximo esplendor entre los años 900 y 1350. En Casas Grandes construyeron la ciudad de Paquimé y desde ahí se empezaron a extender, estableciendo una serie de rutas comerciales que llegaron a alcanzar hasta Mesoamérica, en el centro y sur de México.

Una de las rutas comerciales más importantes de este pueblo, fue la que establecieron hacia la costa del golfo de California y océano Pacífico. Para establecer ésta, los paquimé utilizaron la parte norte de la Sierra Tarahumara, específicamente la región de las barrancas del actual municipio de Madera, conformada por la cuenca del río Papigochi y su barranca principal de Huápoca (1620 metros de profundidad). A lo largo de estas barrancas fueron construyendo una serie de pequeños pueblos en el interior de grandes cavidades y abrigos rocosos localizados en sitios bastante abruptos y aislados. A estos sitios les llamamos "cuevas con casas".

Durante un lapso de más de 300 años, entre los años 1000 y 1350, los paquimé de la sierra florecieron y mantuvieron las rutas comerciales con la costa. Fueron cientos los sitios de cuevas con casas y en algunos de ellos llegaron a habitar hasta 200 personas o un poco más. Estos grupos serranos, para mantenerse, practicaban la caza, la recolección y la agricultura. Esta última la hacían en terrazas y construían graneros para almacenar el maíz y las calabazas.

Hacia el año 1350 se inició la decadencia de esta cultura, al ser invadido su territorio por grupos nómadas, quienes les destruyeron su ciudad. Aproximadamente en el año 1450 Paquimé fue abandonada definitivamente y con esto desapareció la cultura al dispersarse sus grupos. Asimismo, al ser abandonadas las rutas comerciales que alimentaban la ciudad de Paquimé, los sitios de cuevas con casas dejaron de tener razón de ser y fueron abandonados y olvidados. Pasarían muchos años antes de que se volviera a saber de ellos.

Un poco más de cien años después de que esta cultura se extinguiera, los primeros españoles llegaron a las ruinas de Casas Grandes. Sin embargo, no fue sino hasta finales del siglo XIX cuando con las famosas exploraciones de Carl Lumholtz en la Sierra Tarahumara, se tuvieron las primeras noticias de los pueblos subterráneos de los paquimé serranos. En su libro "El México Desconocido", Lumholtz nos describe una docena de sitios de cuevas con casas, destacando el sitio de Cuarenta Casas, actualmente turístico. En los siguientes años la entrada esporádica de arqueólogos fue dando noticia de algunos sitios más.

A principios de 1995 inicié una serie de exploraciones geográficas en el municipio de Madera. Pronto empecé a encontrar numerosos sitios arqueológicos de cuevas con casas que no se hallaban registrados y al parecer estaban olvidados desde el tiempo mismo en que los paquimé los abandonaron. Empezaron a ser tantos que decidí hacer exploraciones sistemáticas en la zona para ir registrándolos, cartografiándolos y documentándolos. Después de cuatro años de exploraciones encontré un poco más de 100 sitios de gran interés, destacando la región del valle del Hongo en donde se encuentran las cuevas del Hongo, las Jarillas, del Hechicero, del Sol, de las Palmas, Cabeza del Aguila, además de otras partes de gran interés como la cueva de la Ranchería, cueva de los Apaches, cueva de las Siete Estrellas, cueva de la Momia, cuevas del Boruco, cueva de Casa Blanca y cueva del Venado.

Fueron decenas de barrancas a las que fui penetrando para sacar del olvido estos antiguos pueblos, cada descubrimiento fue fascinante. Ante mí fueron apareciendo las cavidades con sus casas de adobe y piedra y techos de troncos de pino y táscate, en algunos casos eran conjuntos de hasta 50 habitaciones con tres niveles. Encontramos las famosas ollas policromadas, con sus dibujos y diseños tan hermosos y característicos, localizamos momias como testimonios de antiguos entierros y ceremonias funerarias. Ante nosotros apareció parte de ese mundo paquimé en los vestigios de su cultura material. Vimos sus viejos graneros y terrazas para cultivar, nos topamos con sus sandalias y petates, metates y puntas de flechas. Además, todos estos descubrimientos los encontramos en un mundo de impresionantes barrancas, sitios difíciles de llegar pero llenos de parajes hermosos, con cascadas y manantiales, ríos y bosques, cielo y estrellas. Terminó de enamorarme esta región cuando me topé con los jabalíes y los cholugos, cuando pude seguir los venados y rastrear las huellas de los osos, escuchar el llamado de los guajolotes y despertarme con el canto de los zenzontles.

Los hallazgos llegaron a ser tan importantes que pronto recibí un motivante apoyo del Gobierno del Estado de Chihuahua para explorar y descubrir. En realidad yo no fui el verdadero descubridor de estos sitios, muchos de ellos fueron encontrados antes que mi por los buscadores de tesoros; vándalos y saqueadores, mismos que han estado ocasionando un daño tremendo a este patrimonio, aproximadamente el 90 % de los sitios que he encontrado hasta la fecha muestran un saqueo y destrucción del 10 al 80 %, e incluso algunos sitios fueron destruidos en su totalidad. Pronto me di cuenta de que si no hacemos algo rápido, los sitios desaparecerán antes de que puedan ser estudiados y conocidos. Así que lo primero que hice fue publicar un libro en donde, además de dar a conocer los hallazgos, hago una denuncia pública para que se detenga la destrucción y el saqueo y las autoridades intervengan. Actualmente estamos haciendo esfuerzos para que toda la región de cuevas con casas sea declarada área natural protegida, al mismo tiempo estamos iniciando en Gobierno del Estado un proyecto turístico que involucre a la comunidad de Madera como una opción económica y que ayude a conservar los sitios, los promueva, se lleguen a restaurar y estudiar. La idea es que protejamos y conservemos el patrimonio que nos heredaron los paquimé y pueda ser disfrutado por propios y visitantes a través de un proyecto económico sustentable.

Hasta la fecha continuo con las exploraciones y siguen apareciendo nuevos sitios de cuevas con casas, de hecho no he explorado ni la mitad del territorio de las barrancas del municipio de Madera y tengo en lista de espera un centenar de sitios por verificar.

Casa Grandes – Nuevo Casas Grandes

El valle de Casas Grandes se localiza en la región noroeste del estado de Chihuahua. Su composición geográfica esta dividida por la Sierra Madre Occidental que ocupa la parte sur del municipio y la mesa central que ocupa la parte norte del mismo, lo cual produce una mezcla de paisajes de montañas, praderas y desiertos, que se conjugan en una misma región enmarcando sus bellos atractivos turísticos.

Su Historia: Los primeros españoles arribaron en 1565 con la expedición de Francisco de Ibarra procedente de Durango. A su llegada Baltazar de Obregón, encargado de llevar la bitácora, describe a Paquimé como "una ciudad que parece haber sido construida por los antiguos romanos", y hace mención del nombre "Paquimé" que era como le llamaban los pobladores de la región en ese tiempo y que indudablemente no eran los descendientes directos de los constructores de tan magnífica obra arquitectónica. A partir de 1661 los franciscanos comenzaron la evangelización construyendo el Convento de San Antonio de Padua de Casas Grandes. Los indígenas del lugar no aceptaron la evangelización y en una ocasión organizaron un juego de pelota que aprovecharon para hacer una rebelión sin tener mucho éxito. En 1668 los colonos españoles comenzaron a solicitar autorización para trasladarse a otra parte, sin embargo este cambio no se dio hasta 1686 cuando se construyó el Templo de San Felipe y Santiago de Janos, al norte de Casas Grandes. A finales del siglo XVIII, el entonces Comandante General de la Nueva Vizcaya, Coronel Teodoro de Croix, estableció una colonia militarizada como apoyo a la línea de presidios construidos para proteger la empresa española del constante ataque de los apaches.

El florecimiento de la población se dio a fines del siglo XIX y principio del XX cuando se exterminó a los apaches y se puso en funcionamiento el ferrocarril. Sus principales actividades económicas fueron la explotación de la madera de la Sierra y las minas de San Pedro Corralitos. En 1875 arribaron a la región los primeros colones mormones procedentes del norte de Estados Unidos.

A partir de la introducción del ferrocarril se creó una división en la comunidad y hubo muchas familias que decidieron mudarse y establecerse alrededor de la estación del tren, formando una nueva comunidad que se fundó formalmente en 1923 con el nombre de Nuevo Casas Grandes y que actualmente cuenta con una población y vida económica mucho mayor. A partir de la década de los 60's se introdujeron varias colonias menonitas que se trasladaron de los alrededores de ciudad Cuauhtémoc.

Ubicación: Su cabecera municipal es Casas Grandes, localizada a 321 km. al noroeste de la ciudad de Chihuahua y a 282 km. al suroeste de Ciudad Juárez en la frontera norte del estado. Su altitud es de 1450 mts. snm y su temperatura oscila entre los –10° C en el invierno y los 35° en el verano.

Entre los principales atractivos de esta región se encuentran: Paquimé: Situada en el hermoso valle de Casas Grandes. Es la zona arqueológica más importante del norte de México. Ciudad prehispánica de urbanización asombrosa que floreció entre los años 900 y 1300 de nuestra era. Para cuando llegaron los primeros españoles a estas tierras, ya

tenía casi doscientos años abandonada. Sus edificios constaban de hasta cinco pisos, con alcobas y escalates interiores. Este sitio se caracterizó por sus puertas en forma de "T", su sistema de abastecimiento y distribución de agua así como por la producción de alfarería policromada.

Museo de las Culturas del Norte: Invaluable joya museografica, recientemente construida por el Instituto Nacional de Antropología e Historia ubicada justo frente a la zona arqueológica de Paquimé. Este museo nos muestra la evolución de los pobladores del norte de México y sur de los Estados Unidos en distintas etapas a través de un excelente guión apoyado de una serie de piezas originales, ilustraciones, maquetas y videos de la región.

Colonias Dublán y Juárez: Habitadas por Mormones quienes por motivos religiosos tuvieron que emigrar del estado de Utah en Estados Unidos de Norteamérica, desde fines del siglo pasado, son sumamente conservadores en sus tradiciones y costumbres, aún podemos ver sus viejas casonas en colonias típicamente norteamericanas.

Colonia El Capulin: Singular sitio escogido por inmigrantes Menonitas de ascendencia Canadiense a quienes se les considera por su religiosa dedicación al trabajo como los mejores granjeros del mundo. Este grupo étnico se mantiene más apegado a sus tradiciones que los menonitas avecindados en el centro del estado, ya que a la fecha no utilizan vehículos de motor ni escuchan el radio, entre otras costumbres.

Hacienda de San Diego: Está situada a 25 kms. al sur de Casas Grandes, se trata de una de las 30 haciendas propiedad del General Luis Terrazas, quien llegó a ser propietario de una buena parte del estado de Chihuahua. La bien conservada construcción data de 1902.

Juan Mata Ortíz: Está situado a 35 kms. al sur de Casas Grandes, es el centro artesanal alfarero más importante del norte de México, la mayoría de sus habitantes se dedican a la elaboración de finisima cerámica de estilo Paquimé, misma que ha obtenido renombre internacional gracias a las distinciones que merecidamente se le han otorgado entre otros al maestro Juan Quezada, redescubridor de la tradición y técnica ancestral en la elaboración de las bellas piezas.

El Arroyo de los Monos: Está situado a 35 kms. al sureste de Casas Grandes. Este sitio presenta gran cantidad de petrograbados, y es de especial interés para la fotografía. Los dibujos en este pequeño cañón son alusivos principalmente a motivos de cacería y animales de la región.

Cueva de la Olla: Ubicada a 75 kms. al suroeste de la Ciudad de Casas Grandes, en este sitio arqueológico se encontraron vestigios más antiguos que la ciudad de Paquimé, pertenece al grupo del Valle de las Cuevas. En el interior de una cavidad natural se encuentra un enorme granero en forma de olla que fue utilizado por sus moradores en forma comunal para el almacenamiento de algunos alimentos.

Sugerencias para Visitar Nuevo Casas Crandes – Casas Grandes

Mormones y Menonitas: Para lograr combinar a estas dos culturas se puede visitar Colonia Dublán en donde después de dar un recorrido por este antiguo barrio lleno de grandes casonas, podemos llegar a una de estas que actualmente ha sido transformada en un agradable restaurante. Posteriormente se sigue hacia el norte 30 km, en donde existe un entronque a la derecha que nos lleva por un camino de terracería hacia el Capulín, conformado por una gran colonia menonita. En este lugar podemos admirar como estos grandes agricultores trabajan el campo así como su forma de vida (este recorrido dura aproximadamente 90 min).

Los artesanos de Mata Ortíz: Este recorrido inicia en Casas Grandes continuando hacia el sur con rumbo a Colonia Juárez que es una antigua colonia mormona en donde se encuentra una de las instituciones académicas más importantes de la región, conocida como Academia Juárez. Esta comunidad nos permite admirar los huertos de manzana y durazno que la rodean, ofreciendo un contrastante paisaje que muestra como a través de los años el empeño de sus habitantes sigue haciendo de esta región una de las principales productoras en el país. A 10 km. al sur de Colonia Juárez se encuentra la Hacienda de San Diego, que data de principios de siglo, vale la pena detenerse un momento para admirar su sobria construcción. Continuando 5 km. al sur por el mismo camino nos lleva al pueblito de Mata Ortíz en donde se puede visitar las viejas casas de adobe en donde viven los grandes artesanos del lugar. Si hay suerte podemos ver como trabajan la alfarería y su decoración y bien comprar piezas recientemente trabajadas por estos hábiles artistas (este recorrido dura aproximadamente 3 hrs.).

Paquimé y el Museo de las Culturas del Norte: A sólo 1 km. de Casas Grandes se localiza este impresionante sitio arqueológico que muestra la alta ingeniería arquitectónica que ésta gran civilización utilizó para la construcción tanto de sus sitios ceremoniales como de sus casas habitación. Este lugar consta actualmente de 14 recintos, 2 centros ceremoniales y una cancha para juego de pelota. Justo frente a Paquimé se encuentra el Museo de las Culturas del Norte que es un complemento esencial para comprender la forma de vida de los antiguos pobladores de la región, a través de la tecnología actual (este recorrido dura aproximadamente 2 hrs.).

Otros sitios a visitar: El Cañón de los Monos que ofrece un espectáculo de petrograbados en un pequeño cañón lleno de vegetación desértica (este recorrido dura dos horas aproximadamente).

El Valle de las Cuevas: Para visitar este lugar es necesario tomarse todo el día y llevar comida para día de campo. En este lugar podremos encontrar los vestigios más antiguos de la región como lo son la Cueva de la Olla y la Cueva de las Golondrinas entre otros (le recomendamos llevar un guía local).

Madera

El municipio de Madera se localiza al norte de la Sierra Madre Occidental, en la parte Noroeste del estado de Chihuahua. Su composición geográfica se presenta bastante variada, contrastando las mesetas y planicies con las barrancas y montañas, todas ellas rodeadas de una intensa vegetación boscosa de pinos y encinos, donde comienza la formación del sistema de barrancos más amplio del mundo, destacando la barranca del rio Papigochi, conocida en Madera como río Sírupa o Huápoca.

Su Historia: Tal y como se menciona en la descripción arqueológica de la región, en Madera existieron distintos asentamientos humanos con cerca de dos mil años de antigüedad, los cuales albergaron diversos grupos étnicos, destacando los que conformaron la cultura Paquimé.

A la llegada de los primeros españoles los indígenas que habitaban la región principalmente, eran los Jovas, que obviamente no eran los descendientes de aquella civilización que dejara tan impresionantes vetigios en las cuevas de los grandes acantilados, como testimonio de su existencia. Las primeras misiones Jesuitas llegaron a fines del siglo XVII a fundar centros en Nahuérachi y Sírupa siendo éstos sitios destruidos por una rebelión hacia 1690.

Posteriormente hacia 1728 se localizaron las primeras minas en la cercanía de Guaynopa iniciándose propiamente la colonización de la region de Madera. A principios de siglo se iniciaron los primeros aserraderos en el paraje conocido como Ciénaga de San Pedro que poco después pasaría a ser la población de San Pedro Madera.

Fundación: El norteamericano William C. Green obtuvo la concesión maderera y creó la empresa Sierra Madre Land & Lumber Company dando gran impulso económico a la region. En 1906 se introdujo el tren a la region, asimismo durante el porfiriato se creó en el municipio de Madera uno de los latifundios mas grandes de México y que sobrevivió hasta 1952, el de Babícora que perteneciera el influyente periodista William Randolph Hearst.

Localización: Su cabecera municipal es Cd. Madera, se localiza a 276 kms. al noroeste de la Cd. de Chihuahua pasando por Cuauhtémoc, Guerrero Matachi y Temósachi y a 536 km.deCiudad Juárez vía Casas Grandes. Su altitud es de 2,112 mts. snm con temperaturas que oscilan entre los −15° y los 30° grados centígrados.

Atractivos Turísticos: Esta región esta llena de bellezas naturales y sitios arqueológicos con diversas manifestaciones arquitectónicas de singular característica así como pequeñas aldeas bien conservadas dentro de cavidades naturales ubicadas en escarpadas cañadas. Recomendamos visitar los siguientes sitios naturales y arqueológicos.

Cuarenta Casas: Ubicado a 54 kms. al norte de Madera por carretera pavimentada. Este importante sitio consiste en un conjunto de casas y habitaciones de adobe construidas bajo el abrigo de una gran cavidad natural en muy buen estado de conservación, con características arquitectónicas muy similares a Paquimé, su última ocupación ocurrió hacia el siglo XII, que se cree fue utilizado como uno de los puntos intermedios de las rutas comerciales que fueron establecidas entre Paquimé y las costas del Océano Pacifico.

Presa Peñitas: Esta laguna artificial se encuentra a sólo 12 km. Al norte de Madera, está rodeada de bosque y es el sitio ideal para pescar o acampar. Durante el invierno, se llena de la algarabía de las grullas y los gansos blancos que emigran de Canadá, ofreciendo una fabuloso espectáculo visual y auditivo.

Complejo Mogollón: Se localiza a 33 kms. al Oeste de Madera por un camino de terracería (una hora de distancia). Este sitio consta de catorce habitaciones en perfecto estado de conservación comprendidas en dos recintos denominados "La Cueva de la Serpiente" y "El Nido de Aguila". La espectacularidad de este sitio se debe a su ubicación, ya que está enclavado al borde un acantilado rodeado de vegetación boscosa y hermosos paisajes.

Cueva Grande: Se localiza a 66 kms. al oeste de Madera por el mismo camino que nos lleva al Complejo Mogollón (45 minutos del complejo). Este sitio muestra otro aspecto distinto de los asentamientos de la Cultura Mogollón ya que se encuentra en una enorme cueva que contiene en su interior un total de ocho recintos con construciones de dos niveles. En época de lluvias se forma una pequeña cascada de la cueva que le de una singular belleza.

Aguas Termales de Huapoca: (48 kms. al oeste, 75 minutos) este manantial rodeado de hermosos paisajes nos permite un reconfortante descanso en aguas termales, después de haber efectuado un espectacular recorrido por la Cueva Grande y el conjunto Mogollón.

Agua Caliente Sírupa: Uno de los manantiales de agua termal más hermosos de la Sierra Tarahumara. Consta de tres brotaderos en el arroyo de Sírupa muy cerca del río del mismo nombre. El agua brota generosa de sendas grietas, en una de ellas forma una pequeña cascada, hay pozas estratégicamente situadas donde es posible tomar on reconfortante baño. Está situado a 60 kms al sur de Madera por el camino de terracería que va al mineral de los Dolores. En sus cercanías se encuentra la antigua hacienda de Sírupa y el sitio arqueológico de La Rancheria.

Puente Colgante de Huapoca: Se encuentra a 48 km. al oeste de Madera por el camino de terracería que va a la Cueva Grande. Construido desde la década de los 50s, sobre el río Huapoca o Sírupa, nos permite apreciar bellas vistas en una parte que se encañona entre paredes rocosas verticales.

Sugerencias para Visitar Ciudad Madera

Paisaje y Arqueología: Este recorrido inicia visitando la Presa Peñitas ya sea para admirar la belleza de su paisaje sobre todo en los meses de invierno que las aves migratorias ofrecen un colorido espectáculo, o bien en primavera y verano para pescar o pasear en bote. Por el mismo camino se continúan 42 km al norte para tomar el entronque a la izquierda que nos lleva al sitio arqueológico Cuarenta Casas. Para llegar hasta las construcciones es necesario caminar 1.5 km entre bajadas y subidas, que bien vale la pena recorrer. Duración: 3 hr aproximadamente.

Arqueología y Naturaleza: Este recorrido inicia por un camino de terracería lleno de una intensa vegetación boscosa en las faldas de la Sierra Madre Occidental. El primer sitio a visitar serí el conjunto Mogollón constituido por las Cuevas de la Serpiente y el Nido de Aguila, ambas ubicadas en altos acantilados. De este lugar se continúan 30 km hacia el oeste para llegar al lugar conocido como la Cueva Grande que es una enorme cueva en un cerro que contiene una serie de construcciones en su interior. El último sitio es las aguas termales de Huapoca en donde podemos tomar un placentero baño en sus posas naturales, reconfortante después de haber efectuado la visita a los sitios arqueológicos.

Otros sitios a visitar. Hacienda de Nahuerachi: A sólo 10 km. al sureste de Madera se encuentra una antigua construcción que tiene sus orígenes desde fines del siglo XVII con la fundación de la Misión del mismo nombre. La Hacienda se encuentra en ruinas que aún muestran el lugar donde comenzaron los primeros asentamientos de los españoles. En 1690 este lugar fue testigo de una violenta rebelión indígena (este recorrido dura 45 min aproximadamente).

Misión de Tres Ojitos: Se llega continuando 20 km al sur por este camino, en donde el Padre Jesús Espronceda es el corazón de la misma, ya que es el guía constructor, artesano, industrial, consejero espiritual y artista.

En este lugar podemos encontrar productos elaborados por los lugareños como son: jamón, chorizo, tocino y demás derivados del cerdo, además de la hospitalidad de so gente.

Aguas Termales de Sirupa: Uno de los manantiales más bonitos de la región. Consta de tres grietas de donde brota el agua, formando en una de ellas una pequeña cascada con posas naturales propias para tomar un reconfortante baño. Este lugar se localiza 60 km al sur de Cd. Madera por un camino de terracería (3 horas y media).

Club de Pesca El Táscate : Este lugar es ideal para la pesca de trucha arcoiris, comidas campestres y campamentos. Se localiza a 20 minutos de Cd.Madera.

Horarios de Sitios Arqueológicos de 9:00 A.M. a 4:00 P.M. Por lo extenso de los recorridos le recomendamos visitar estos sitios por la mañana.

Reseña histórica del Circuito Ruta de Villa

Francisco Villa nació el 5 de junio de 1878 en San Juan del Río en Durango. Se unió con el movimiento antireeleccionista encabezado por Francisco I. Madero contra el gobierno de Porfírio Díaz, en Chihuahua surgieron varios grupos guerrilleros, Abraham González invita a Villa a sumarse al movimiento y posteriormente conoce a Madero con el cual se confiesa y obtiene su confianza. Se distingue como jefe en las batallas de San Andrés (Riva Palacio), Santa Isabel (General Trías), Santa Rosalía (Camargo) y Las Escobas. Une sus fuerzas militares con Pascual Orozco, obteniendo la toma de Ciudad Juárez y provocando la renuncia del General Díaz a la Presidencia de la República.

En 1912 Orozco se revela contra Madero, mientras que Villa, se incorpora a las filas de la fuerza militar llamada División del Norte Federal. Ataca con éxito Bustillos, Casas Grandes, San Andrés y otras ciudades como Avilés, Lerdo, Gómez Palacio y Torreón. En septiembre estos grupos armados se constituyen como DIVISION DEL NORTE CONSTITUCIONALISTA al mando del General Francisco Villa, se le uniría más tarde un gran estratega militar, el General Felipe Angeles.

Villa fue Gobernador Provisional de Chihuahua y durante su mandato, mandó imprimir billetes, embargó tiendas, abarató los precios del maíz, frijol y la carne; abrió escuelas dotándolas de material didáctico, decretó el establecimiento del Banco del Estado y asumió funciones federales en materia de telégrafos y ferrocarriles. Expulsó a varios grupos de españoles acusándolos de ayudar a Victoriano Huerta.

A principios de 1914 vuelven los enfrentamientos y Villa toma las ciudades de Ojinaga, Torreón y Saltillo. En junio tras la cruenta batalla de la toma de Zacatecas, desobedece las órdenes de Carranza como Primer Jefe y desde ese momento, las relaciones entre ambos se agudizan y se complican.

Carranza asume la presidencia interina de México y Villa lo limita en sus poderes, lo presiona al convocar la Convención de Generales y Gobernadores para señalar la celebración de elecciones democráticas y formular un programa de gobierno. Al no respetarse acuerdos mutuos, en 1914 estalla otra vez un conflicto armado, con el pretexto que en Sonora, Villa apoyaba al Gobernador Maytorena, mientras que Obregón, Hill, Elias Calles y Alvarado formaban otro grupo político.

Desmoralizado por las derrotas de Celaya, de Trinidad, de León y Aguascalientes, se vuelca en ira al darse cuenta que las municiones estaban defectuosas, por lo que, el 9 de marzo de 1916 al mando de 400 hombres, ataca la población norteamericana de Columbus, buscando a los comerciantes que le habían vendido "el parque". Provocando que el ejército norteamericano lo persiguiera por la región de Chihuahua y Durango, con el consentimiento de Carranza, en la llamada "Expedición Punitiva" comandada por el General Pershing, sin lograr atraparlo. De 1917 a 1920 desarrolló una guerra de guerrillas, limitándose debido a la escasez de las armas y recursos.

Como fruto del movimiento de Agua Prieta, Adolfo de la Huerta asume la Presidencia interina del país, logrando llegar a un acuerdo de rendición con Villa. Se retira a la Hacienda de Canutillo en Durango, donde el Gobierno Federal le cedió la hacienda en propiedad y con autorización para tener una escolta. Murió acribillado junto con su escolta en una emboscada, muy cerca del centro de la ciudad de Hidalgo del Parral, mientras viajaba en su automóvil Dodge 1922, el 20 de julio de 1923.

Las Majestuosas Barrancas

Se dice que en el Estado de Chihuahua hay cinco barrancas más hondas que el Gran Cañón del Colorado. El primer descenso y exploración de dos de las más estrechas y profundas se realizó in 1986. Llama la atención que estos increíbles abismos no hayan sido documentados en la edad moderna. El desarrollo de las técnicas exploratorias de las barrancas las ha hecho accesibles para la investigación y documentación.

Durante años las grandes barrancas de México habían sido reconocidas como unas de las áreas mas salvajes, abruptas e interesantes de la América Septentrional. Partes de ellas habían sido exploradas desde 1890 por Carl Lumholtz. Sin embargo, en cuanto yo conozco, no se había hecho un esfuerzo por completar el inventario de su profundidad "desde el nivel del suelo." Las siguientes líneas ilustran la prufundidad fisica de las barrancas estudiadas (datos proporcionados por cortesía del Dr. Robert H. Schmidt).

El Rio Verde y la Barranca de Sinforosa

Descripción General. El Rio Verde es el más grande de los tres ríos que drenan la Sierra Tarahumara central, con el más alto indice anual de agua. Es el más remoto y difícil de alcanzar de los tres ríos: Urique, Batopilas y Verde. Por su lejanía e inaccesibilidad es uno de los menos explorados y documentados de América del Norte. Generalmente se piensa que estos tres ríos han excavado las mayores y más profunas barrancas norteñas, y que éstas conforman el sistema barranqueño más grande del mundo.

La presencia humana ha impactado enormenente y modificado la flora y la fauna de las barrancas, sobre todo con el pastoreo de chivas y ganado. Sin embargo, hay una excepción espectacular en las áreas más estrechas, en donde pristinos boscajes con plantas exóticas, pájaros y mamíferos subsisten a pesar de la cuña humana.

La geología de las barrancas consta primariamente de estratos igneos endurecidos. Estas rocas, excepcionalmente duras, son muy resistentes a la erosión y hacen que el cauce del río se llene de peñascos de tremendas proporciones. El gradiente del río es también extremo, estimando en 120 pies por milla la pendiente promedio en sus partes más angostas.

Familias de tarahumaras y mestizos utilizan las Barrancas. Los tarahumaras y tepehuanes no son tan numerosos ahí, y por lo general se alojan en el tercio superior del cañón. Con todo vimos una familia tarahumara que vivía temporalmente al nivel del río.

Barranca de Urique

Descripción General. Carl Lumholtz escribe que en lengua tarahumara *Urique* significa barranca. Hay alguna confusión respecto a los sitios a los que puede aplicarse este nombre. El Río Urique empieza cerca de Norogachi y corre por dos grandes barrancas antes de confluir en el Río Fuerte. La barranca superior es la del Cobre y la inferior la de Urique. El pueblo de Urique está situado en la porción superior de la barranca homónima, que termina en el Río Fuerte. Pocos saben que abajo de la confluencia de los rios Urique y Fuerte hay un pequeño y hermoso cañón, que yo llamaría el Cañón del Fuerte.

El el pueblo de Tubares están las espléndidas ruinas de una antigua misión. Se dice que en 1968 murió el último Tubar, con el que se extinguió el grupo. Hay que tener cuidado en éste caserío de no aventurarse mas allá del área de la misión. Río abajo de Tubares queda El Realito, un sitio encantador. A unas cinco millas de aní, siguiendo la corriente, hay varios rápidos que terminan en un peligroso salto de agua, según pudimos precisarlo.

Cinco millas adelante de esta cascada está la presa de San Francisco. El río corta un canal a través de la presa sin formar un lago; con todo, la presa misma es un paso obligatorio. Abajo de la presa, en el corazón de la barranca, las aguas del Río Fuerte se deslizan con toda placidez. En otros tiempos hubo allí cocodrilos. En los mapas topográficos está mal señalado el sitio de la presa de San Francisco, que está a día y medio de camino de la estación ferroviaria de Agua Caliente.

Barranca del Cobre

Descripción General. Expediciones anteriores a esta barranca han producido valiosas informaciones. Por su accesibilidad, gracias al ferrocarril y al pueblo maderero de Creel, la Barranca del Cobre ha sido el sitio de muchas expediciones científicas y de aficionados. Se ha intentado bajar hasta el río, pero hay un concenso general de que no conviene hacer un recorrido tradicional por el cauce de esta barranca. Muchas expediciones han fracasado debido a la naturaleza extremadamente pedregoso del lecho del río y por no haber llevado el instrumental técnico apropiado para una topografía.

La Barranca del Cobre es intransitable por sus enormes peñascos y caídas de agua a diez millas río abajo del puente de Umirá. En este sector rocoso el río corre bajo tierra por más de una milla; más adelante el río vuelve a su normalidad como en la Barranca de Sinforosa (ver fotografías). Otras áreas ya se han intentado con lanchas o kayaks. Una de ellas va de El Tejabán hacia abajo del Divisadero, trayecto que se ha descrito como intransitable. Un grupo no tuvo mejor suerte al pretender ir con kayaks inflables del Divisadero al pueblo de Urique.

De Creel a Batopilas

Para llegar a este singular lugar se requiere recorrer uno de los caminos más espectaculares de la sierra; las impresionantes vistas a lo largo del recorrido que toma seis horas le impactarán. Durante el trayecto, se lleva a cabo el descenso al fondo de la barranca, a 500 mts. snm., Batopilas está a sólo 123 kilómetros de Creel. Sin temor a equivocarme, es uno de los pueblos mineros con mayor encanto en la Sierra Tarahumara. En 1708 se inició el pueblo de Batopilas gracias al descubrimiento de ricos yacimientos de plata. A fines del siglo XIX estas minas eran explotadas por una compañía norteamericana. Un exalcalde de la ciudad de Washington, Alexander Sheperd, se decidió a vivir rodeado de la exhuberante belleza del lugar y mandó construir una enorme residencia con las amenidades a las que estaban acostumbrados él y su familia. Batopilas fue la segunda población de toda la República Mexicana en contar con luz eléctrica. (La primera fue la Ciudad de México). El mineral era trasladado a lomo de mula; se cuenta que había ocasiones en que hasta 200 animales cargados a la vez, recorrían las empinadas veredas con rumbo al embarque. Seis kilómetros al sur de Batopilas se encuentra la vieja iglesia de la Misión de Satevó construída por Misioneros Jesuitas a mediados del siglo XVIII para evangelizar a los indios Tubares, -hoy desafortunadamente desaparecidos-. El enorme templo está situado en el fondo de la barranca en un hermoso valle, rodeado de encanto y soledad.

Actualmente, las orgullosas familias, descendientes de aquellos buscadores de minas -que quedaron embrujados por el lugar y llamaron hogar a este sitio-, viven del comercio y recientemente del turismo.

Los Rarámuri o Tarahumaras
by Luis G. Verplancken, S.J.

Este breve escrito no pretende ser un estudio antropológico, ni siquiera un resumen de la cultura tarahumara, ya que existen muchos, algunos muy buenos y también los hay sobre aspectos particulates, como la carrera de bola, su economia y transhumancia, el batari - su bebida ritual, etc. Es simplemente un ensayo basado en vivencias a través de 37 años de convivencia casi ininterrumpida con este pueblo noble, leal a Dios, a sus tradiciones y a su cultura.

Dada la brevedad de este ensayo, lo aqui escrito será sólo una semblanza de algunos aspectos sobresalientes de su cultura sus ritos y sus constumbres, ya que es imposible verter una cultura tan rica en unas cuantas paginas.

Procuraré integrar algunos datos que generalmente interesan al público en general, datos que con frecuencia me pregunta la gente respecto a la cultura indigena de los Tarahumaras, asi como otros aspectos culturales interesantes menos conocidos, su filosofia de la vida, su forma de relacionarse con Dios, con el hombre y su comunidad. Me referiré a ellos como los Rarámuri, - Los Hombres -, como se llaman ellos a si mismos. (Tarahumara no es sino la corrupción de la palabra Rarámuri: Tar'amuri, inversion Tarumari, de ahi Tarahumara.)

Me referiré a lo que pudiéramos llamar un denominador común de los Rarámuri y no a un sitio en particular, ni tampoco a los gentiles o no cristianos (de los que hay algunos grupos), sino a los Rarámuri Pagótuame, - hombres bautizados - como se designan a si mismos y con quienes he tenido el privilegio de convivir.

Antepasados de los Rarámuri

Es probable que los antepasados de los indigenas Tarahumaras hayan llegado del Asia, atravesando el Estrecho de Bering, hace aproximadamente unos quince o vientemil años. Su cultura en esa época era del último Paleolitico y de Primer Neolitco. Estos emigrantes del Asia eran de raza mongoloide. Eran cazadores y Pescadores. Su desarrollo agrícola tuvo lugar en el hemisferio Occidental. El movimiento era hacia el progreso tecnológico. El cultivo del maiz, que ya en la prehistoria se habia desarrollado en América Central y del Sur, revolucionó sus vidas. Miles de años de luchas sociales los dotaron de una intensidad de vida, una forma de existencia, una belleza en las relaciones humanas, una felicidad y una amplitud de personalidad que probablemente el mundo actual no tiene, pese a su superior evolución tecnológica. - Mas cerca de nuestra época, acaso a principios de la era cristiana, descendieron junto con los Aztecas que se establecieron mas al Sur, constituyen, hasta la actualidad una de las más cerradas y puras de todas las tribus indigenas de México. Los hombres son de tez broncinea y fornidos, de pies ligeros y miembros fuertes. (Collier, John, "Indians of the Americas" pp. 17-20.)

Vestido

El traje tipico de los Rarámuri, quizás los más primitivos e intocados por la civilización moderna en México, consiste en un taparrabo conocido comunmente como zapeta, Tagora, sostenido por una faja de lana sujeta con dos vueltas alrededor de la cintura, una banda o turbante, koyera, en la cabeza para mantener el pelo en su lugar, una camisa amplia de algodón, napatza, y huaraches, akaka, en los pies. Antiguamente hechos de cuero y ahora de partes de llantas usadas y correas de cuero curtido para atárselos. Este traje tipico ha ido desaparaciendo en muchas regiones de la Sierra Tarahumara. En el atuendo externo es en lo que más ha influido el contacto con la civilización, principalmente en los hombres, no asi en las mujeres que son mas conservadoras. En ellas es mas lenta la influencia, porque pesa mucho entre ellas el "qué diran" de las demas mujeres de su comunidad.

Ellas usan múltiples faldas amplias, plizadas no solo en la cintura sino también a la mitad y en la parte inferior de la falda, - siputza o sipucha -, preferentemente de telas de algodón, que son menos fácilmente inflamables. Gustan mucho de los colores vivos, muy en especial el rojo y de telas floreadas, pero también es muy común la manta blanca asi mismo de algodón. Sus blusas van siempre sueltas de la cintura, son amplias y sus mangas un poco abajo del codo y muy plizadas al hombro y al puño. En la cabeza, al igual que los hombres, usan la koyera, o bien una pañoleta que en algunas regiones se la atan a la nuca y en otras bajo la barbilla.

En varias regiones ha desaparacido ya totalmente el uso de la kovera, tanto en los hombres como en las mujeres; ellos usan sombrero y ellas sólo la bandana o pañoleta. El color de la kovera no tiene ningún significado, como algunos afirman, lo usan indiferentemente, aunque para las fiestas gustan más de los colores vivos y llamativos. También usan las mujeres un chal o rebozo - gimira -, que les es sumamente util para cargar a sus niños o mercancias en la espalda. Las niñas, - tewekes -, también visten igual que sus mamas y aprenden desde pequeñas a cargar cosas y a sus hermanitos en la espalda con la gimira. En los pies usan huaraches como los hombres, pero es frecuente en algunas regiones ver a muchas de las mujeres con los pies descalzos, lo mismo que a los menores de edad.

Tristes Experiencias

La cultura Rarámuri no puede entenderse sin recurrir a su historia que necesariamente ha influenciado su vida, sus constumbres y su habitat. La experiencia que han vivido en las ultimos siglos, es muy importante para comprender algunos aspectos de su vida actual y su actitud hacia el hombre blanco, de quien siempre han resultado victimas. Ya desde las primeras incursiones de mineros buscadores de oro y plata les obligaron a trabajar en las minas tratándolos como esclavos, les depojaron de sus mejores tierras, y les vieron siempre como a parias e incultos que por el simple hecho de ser conquistados no tenian otro derecho que el de hacer y comportarse de acuerdo a la voluntad de los nuevos amos. Se usó la fuerza militar para sojuzgarlos, hubo levantamientos y rebeliones; al ser masacrados para dominarlos, cambiaron los indigenas de actitud. Algunos optaron por retirarse a lugares mas remotos en donde pudieran gozar de tranquilidad, anque tuvieran que abandonar sus mejores tierras. Otros decidieron por una resistencia pacifica de no agresion, aunque les displace enormemente el trabajar en las minas, porque eso significa entrar dentro del seno de la tierra cerca de donde está reré betéame, el que vive abajo, en contraposición de repá betéame, el que vive arriba, Dios.

Desalojo

La población no indigena (blanca o mestiza), en sesenta años, según los censos, casi se ha duplicado. Además de las tierras que ahora ocupan los Rarámuri en la parte montañosa y en las barrancas, poseían, de acuerdo a los anales de los antiguos misioneros que entraron por primera vez a la región de los Rarámuri en 1606, las fértiles tierras de los enormes valles de: San Pablo Balleza (que fue una de las primeras cabeceras de misión de los jesuitas); San Francisco de Borja (fundada también por los jesuitas con el nombre del sucesor de San Ignacio de Loyola, fundador de los jesuitas); Papigochi (aliora Cd. Guerrero); Tomochi y el gigantesco Valle de Mataclif, lugares todos de misiones o centros indigenas en donde a la fecha no existe ningún Rarámuri si no es de visita o como inmigrante buscando trabajo en algún huerto o rancho. Hace un siglo Carl Lumlioltz, en su estupendo estudio etnografico "El México Desconocido," observa impresionado cómo 'los mexicanos' van desalojando de sus mejores tierras a los indigenas: "Guachochi se halla en la misma mitad de la región de los tarahumaras, bien que los mexicanos se iran apropiado las mejores tierras del alrededor, en donde tienen hoy extensos y fértiles ranchos. Hacia el oriente, rumbo a los pueblos de Tónachi y Lagunitas, la ancha faja de tierra faja de labor y de pasto, hasta el Parral, es ahora exclusivamente propiedad de los mexicanos." (p. 195). "Los indios atribuyen los malos tiempos a la presencia de los blancos, que los han privado de sus tierras y de su libertad . . ." (p. 198). ". . . Habiéndole No dicho - al más rico del pueblo de Tónachi que me simpatizaban los tarahumaras, me contestó: 'pues lléveselos todos, uno por uno.' Lo único que le interesaba de los indios eran sus tierras, de las cuales se habia apropiado ya una buena porción." (p. 227).

Los Rarámuri ven siempre al hombre blanco como un intruso, como un invasor de la tierra que siempre fué de ellos y de la que ellos se sienten parte integrante y no sólo de ella, sino de la naturaleza misma, pues la tierra para todo indigena, de cualquier raza que sea, es parte vital de su vida, porque la tierra es vida para el Rarámuri y es, ademas, el lugar donde los puso Dios. Ese Dios que en la concepción Rarámuri es Padre y Madre al mismo tiempo, (asi lo repiten continuamente los Gobernadores en sus sermones o newésaris). En cambio el hombre blanco, el no Rarámuri, no es hijo del que vive arriba, porque engaña, roba, acumula, despoja, invade sus tierras, es ventajoso en sus tratos, se aprovecha del bosque . . ., estos son los peores pecados de la moral Rarámuri: la no hermandad, la acumulación con el consecuente empobrecimiento del prójimo, el no compartir, contrariamente a sus valores fundamentales que son, entre otros, la fraternidad, la rectitud, la equidad y el compartir. Esta es la experiencia que han vivido por siglos, de ahi el recelo y la eterna desconfianza hacia el hombre blanco. Carl Lumholtz dice: "El Tarahumara, por regla general, no es ladrón . . . Mientras se conserva en su estado nativo, nunca engaña el tarahumara en sus tratos." "Estos - Los Rarámuri - son hijos de Dios y los mexicanos son hijos del diablo . . ." (pp. 241 y 291). Esto último lo dice refiriéndose a lo que piensan los Rarámuri de los blancos y mestizos.

Este despojo de las mejores tierras, que han venido sufriendo los Rarámuri, ha continuado a través de los siglos en grande escala y sigue su curso en forma paulatina pero constante, ha hecho que en la actualidad padezcan hambre, desnutrición y tuberculosis, por ende, la mortalidad infantil tiene porcentajes tan altos. Según Carl Lumholtz, los Rarámuri no padecian hambre como ahora. Su testimonio es contundente: "El clima de la sierra, aunque no tan agradable . . . es en extremo salubre . . . No se conocen alli las enfermedades pulmonares." Despúes repite: "Su resistencia es verdaderamente fenomenal ... El rasgo mas notable de estos indios es la maravillosa salud que tienen y que se les advierte desde luego," (pp. 205 y 239).

En ese tiempo en que poseian todas esas fértiles tierras en abundancia, sin duda que no faltaba tierra de siembra para ningún Rarámuri, ni pasaban hambre como ahora, ni tenian necesidad de pedir ayuda o kótima, (literalmente significa "compartir"), como desgraciadamente tienen que hacerlo ahora en las ciudades dando mala reputación a su raza y aun creando problemas sociales.

Atención de la Salud.
Para atender al derecho humano de la salud de los
Rarámuri, la Misión Tarahumara, se vió en la precisión de establecer tres hospitales en la región. El de Creel se estableció en el año 1965, Ileva el nombre de Clinica Santa Teresita y actualmente cuenta con 65 camas para niños y adultos, 3 médicos, 25 enfermeras y los servicios más indispensables de un hospital: farmacia, laboratorio, quirófanos, Rayos X, maternidad, clinica dental, etc. Anualmente atiende un promedio de 6,000 pacientes en consulta externa y 1,100 hospitalizados, principalmente niños. La atención para los indigenas es prácticamente gratuita. También se atiende a los no indigenas y empleados de Empresas, con lo que hay un pequeño pocentaje de recuperación. El hospital se sostiene de donativos y del producto de venta de artesanias, que los mismos indigenas manufacturan y venden en nuestra tienda: "Artesanias Misión," en el mismo pueblo de Creel.

Hermandad, Cortesia y Respeto
En la filosofia Rarámuri es primordial el respeto a la persona, por lo que los visitantes y turistas deberán también ser respetuosos con ellos y sus tradiciones, como ellos lo son con toda la gente. Valoran más a las personas que a las cosas, al grado de que aun los negocios pasan a segundo término. En su cultura es grave falta de educación el tratar algún negocio o arreglar algún asunto antes de haberse tomado tiempo para saludar y tratar con las personas. Al Ilegar a donde hay gente reunida saludan de mano a cada uno de los presentes asi sea mucha la gente que está reunida, pues el saludo es otro signo caracterfstico de su cortesia y de ese respeto y valorización de las personas sobre las cosas materiales.

En cierta ocasión en una charla con un anciano Rarámuri muy respetado, pues es como un gurú entre su gente, habiéndole preguntado acerca de los grupos de Rarámuris gentiles o no bautizados, simplemente respondió: "creo que son más gentiles aquellos que aman más a las cosas que a las personas," dando a entender que a su juicio eran más paganos los cbabocbi como Ilaman ellos al hombre blanco, al mestizo, que aquellos que nosotros Ilamamos gentiles solo por el hecho de no estar bautizados. O en otras palabras, sentia mas cerca de Dios a aquellos gentiles, por el hecho de ser hermanables y porque, al igual que los Rarámuri Pagótuame, bautizados, de acuerdo a su filosofia y su cultura valoran más a las personas que a las cosas materiales.

Ese valorar a las personas más que a las cosas vale también con sus hijos, a quienes nunca regañan, y desde muy pequeños les dejan la responsabilidad de decidir por ellos mismos. A los doce o trece años ya son considerados como adultos en la comunidad. Parte de esa responsabilidad la adquieren al serles asignados desde pequeñitos, una o dos chivas de las que son dueños absolutos y los padres no pueden disponer de ellas sin la anuencia del niño que es dueño; también las crias de esas chivas que son asignadas perteneceran al nuevo miembro de la familia. De esa manera desde muy pequeños van adquiriendo la admirable responsabilidad que desde muy jóvenes ejercen los

Rarámuri. Lumholtz (ibid) menciona el hecho: "El joven tiene sus propios animales que ha adquirido cuando pequeño, y su padre le da un pedazo de tierra." (p. 266).

El ser hospitalarios con los de su raza, que van de paso o de viaje, y aun con los extraños es también parte de su filosofia de gran respeto a la persona porque el ser hermanables y compartir del alimento que tienen, es para ellos como un deber sagrado y el dejarlo de hacer es como un pecado que no se perdona. Asi, cuando llega uno a sus casas, por ese deber y su cortesia, ofrecen luego algo de pinole, frijoles, tortillas, etc. Entre los Tepehuanes hay un decir común refiriéndose a los Rarámuri, que dice: ". . . cuando vayas entre los Tarahumaras nunca pasarás hambre" (Robles, R.: El Reino de los Rarámuri Pagótuame). Y Lumholtz también dice: "Lo primero que piensa un indio que cae enfermo, es preguntarse: a quién habré ofendido?, qué cosa me habré tomado indebidamente o que habré conservado para mi en vez de darlo? El curandero le dirá que se acuerde de la persona a quien haya negado de comer y el enfermo y su mujer van de casa en casa preguntando: Eres tu a quien no he dado de comer?" (p. 309).

Todo esto no es mas que el resultado de su respeto valorización que tienen de las personas, pues en medio de su probreza saben compartir. Su cortesía esta también respaldada por ese aprecio de las personas. "En su lenguaje tienen la palabra 'rekó' equivalente a nuestras expresiones 'Sirvase Ud.; Tenga Ud. la bondad; Haga Ud. favor,' etc., la cual es de uso constantes." (Lumholtz C., p. 254). En el vocabulario indígena no existen las palabras altisonantes, por lo que tienen que recurrir a las mexicanas que han aprendido de los 'chabochi'.

Convivencia Comunitaria

Es notoria su fraternidad, convivencia, servicialidad y ayuda mutua en todas sus faenas agrícolas, en la construcción de una casa o un cerco, o en cualquier labor que requiera del trabajo de varias personas; a cambio, se comparte algo de pinole o tortillas y frijoles. El principal atractivo de esas jornadas es el Teswino - barari -, su típica cerveza de maíz. "Nadie puede ver atendido su campo sin antes proveerse de bastante teswino, que es la única remuneración que reciben los que le ayudan." (Lumholtz C. p. 250).

Evangelización

El impacto de los primeros misioneros en la vida religiosa de los Rarámuri fue muy grande, ya que los mismos misioneros encontraron que los indigenas tenian muy buena disposición y coherencia entre sus vidas y la vida Cristiana. El único punto que todos los misioneros antiguos aun mencionan como negativa (y en buena parte estoy de acuerdo con ellos) fue el excesivo uso del teswino en sus fiestas y ceremonias, principalmente por las consecuencias de la misma embriaguez en esas ocasiones. Esto no quiere decir que fue fácil la evangelización en sus principios, de hecho hubo resistencia y oposiciones fuertes de algunos de sus dirigentes y en grupo, en contra de los misioneros, ya que, al ser extranjeros, les asociaban con los invasores buscadores de oro, que llegaron prácticamente al mismo tiempo, casi siempre acompañados de fuerzas armadas. Eso obviamente dificultó la evangelización y en los levantamientos llegaron a martirizar a algunos misioneros.

Hubo misiones florecientes en muchos puntos de la región ocupada por los Rarámuri. Que empezaron desde la primera Ilegada del Padre Juan Font, en 1607, hasta 1767, en que por decreto del Rey Carlos III de España, todos los Jesuitas fueron expulsados de sus dominios de Latinoamérica, lo cual incluyó necesariamente a los Jesuitas que laboraban en esta región.

La expulsión de los Jesuitas misioneros significó el abandono de las misiones y el dejar a los indigenas totalmente a merced de las manos voraces de los invasores que paulatinamente les despojaron de sus mejores tierras hasta hacerlos desaparecer por completo de algunas regiones como indicamos mas arriba. Por otra parte, ése abandóno que no pudo ser suplido debidamente por los Franciscanos, por haberles sido hostil el Siglo XIX con las guerras de independencia, falta de subsidios y de personal, (Almada). Asi, quedaron practicamente abandonadas las Misiones, con escasa suplencia de unos cuantos sacerdotes diocesanos y, a finales de Siglo, de los Padres josefinos, con cabecera en Cusárare.

Cristianismo en Moldes Rarámuri

Este abandóno por parte del clero, ese estar solos, durante casi siglo y medio, les dejó en libertad para reinterpretar lo que habian aprendido de los Misioneros y vaciar su cristianismo en sus propios moldes de símbolos ritos, abandonando lo que nada les decía y conservando y adaptando a su expresión cultural simbólica el resto, cosa que no hubiera sido posible que hicieran los misioneros con su mentalidad occidental y además conceptual. Para los indigenas las enseñanzas que aprendieron entonces y aprenden ahora de sus gobernadores o siriames, más que definicinies o conceptos, son coherencia entre vida y enseñanzas, en otras palabras, ellos no saben dar razón verbal o conceptual de las enseñanzas que han aprendido, si no que deben hacerlo en forma de testimonio en la vida misma.

Su Teología

Su teologia no es un tratado, ni un dogma o conceptos abstractos, de ahí la dificultad para entenderles quienes estamos acostumbrados a definiciones y respuestas precisas. Ellos tienen una "Religiosidad Popular" muy suya, muy rica, sorprendentemente ortodoxa en todo lo básico, que aprenden en la vida misma, en su relación con la comunidad, en los nawésaris de sus siríames, en su constante relación con Dios. Los ancianos, los owirúames (doctores y guías espirituales) y los Siríames van guiando y enseñando al pueblo, a la comunidad, esa teologia Tarahumara en la prátctica de la vida misma. En sus ceremonias, variados ritos y fiestas, siempre al paso de los acontecimientos de la vida diaria y nunca en tratados áridos, desconectados de la vida, como los nuestros. Por ello, para entenderles y comprender su teologia, el camino no puede ser el preguntarles sobre sus conceptos teológicos, puesto que jamás los formulan; el único camino es la convivencia con ellos y observar su vida y sus actos, sus múltiples fiestas, ceremonias y ritos, llenos de simbolismo. (Robles, R. ibid.)

Su verdad de hijos de Dios está en la práctica de su vida. Sus hechos son la verdad, verdad que necesariamente evoluciona y se acomoda a la vida diaria, que también cambia, siguiendo siempre una pauta, en consonancia con su tradición; cambios que se dan en la practica de su vicia y no por disposiciones teóricas. Esa es su religión en el ejercicio de la vida diaria, nunca en conceptos. (Robles, R. Ibid.)

Ritos y Danzas

Cuando por primera vez se conoce a los Rarámuri, podriamos pensar que su cultura o sus ritos ceremoniales, son una mezcla incompressible de signos paganos y cristianos y asi suelen citarlos quienes les ven u observan superficialmente. Muy en concreto los juzgan asi la mayoria de los mestizos de la región, los 'chabochi', 'barbados', como les Ilaman los Rarámuri, sin entender que para la cultura tarahumara, que no especula, el rito, abstraido en símbolos, es lo importante. Asi su oración es ritualmente simbolizada más en la danza que en oraciones vocales; el saludo reverente a la cruz a las imágenes de los Santos, lo simbolizan sigándose en la cara y rotando el cuerpo hacia la izquierda.

Para nuestra mentalidad conceptual nos pueden resultar o nos resultan incomprensibles sus expresiones simbólicas rituales. Encontramos desde nuestra ortodoxia Occidental contradicciones e incoherencias que nos desconciertan, pero a ellos, que no suelen especular sobre esas cosas, no les causan ningún conflicto. A nosotros nos parece una incoherencia ingénua el que ofrezcan comida a sus muertos, pero para ellos es un deber de fraternidad y de ayudar a la persona que ya se fué y que va de camino. Al que ya llamó el que vive arriba," al que ya necesitó Onoruame, para que tenga energias con el olor de la comida, de la que consume su fuerza alimenticia y ya no servir para nutrir a los vivientes.

Para ellos, los Rarámuri Cristianos, desde antiguo, el Sol es el simbolo de Dios, Onoruame, el que es Padre-Madre pero es único (siempre reiteran los gobernadores en sus sermones la idea monoteista de Tata-rioshi, (del Castellano Tata-Dios), del que se saben ellos los hijos, y con quien sienten un deber u obligación de obedecer y de ayudar para que no prevalezca el mal sobre el bien, como veremos mas adelante. Con esto no quiero decir que fueran adoradores del sol, ni que lo sean ahora, sino por el contrario, que el sol es simplemente el simbolo de Dios. Existen también otros mitos y leyendas acerca de la luna y las estrellas, que no tocaremos aqui, Cfr. Lumholtz (pp. 292-317).

Con la danza piden perdón, piden la lluvia, dan gracias por ella, agradecen las cosechas, ayudan a repá betáme, al que vive arriba, para que no pueda ser vencido y predomine sobre el que vive abajo, rerá betáme, el diablo, y asi prevalezca el bien sobre el mal. Lumholtz dice al prepósito: . . . continuó despúes persiguiéndome la lluvia, con gran complacencia de los indios que visitaba quienes durante largo tiempo habian estado haciendo rogativas y danzas porque lloviera." (p. 199) "La danza no sólo expresa solicitud de lluvia y de vida, sino también peticiones a los dioses (?) para que libren de todo mal, de todo género de daños, a los hombres, a los animales y a las cosechas." (p. 326).

Ancestralmente poseian ya la danza ritual del Yúmari o Tutuguri, en la que hay ofrendas de alimentos a Dios, que en el momento culminante del ofrecimiento, wiroma, ofrecen a Dios hacia los cuatro puntos cardinales y, del que Dios se alimenta con su olor y bendice los alimentos. El rito quizá es el mismo ancestral, pero en su mentalidad de sentirse y saberse hijos del único y verdadero Dios, Padre-Madre. Ahora lo han cristianizado y lo llevan a cabo en la hermanidad de los hijos de Dios, conglutinando asi a la comunidad de quienes son hermanos por ser hijos de un mismo Padre-Madre.

Otra danza, la de los Matachines, que no era autóctona, sino introducida por los misioneros, fue aceptada por los Rarámuri y a tal grado integrada en sus ritos ceremoniales, que es ya una danza autóctona en su cultura y en sus fiestas, principalmente en las del calendario católico: Guadalupe, Navidad, Epifanía, Corpus, Candelaria, fiestas patronales y otras, pero también incluyen los matachines en muchos de sus ritos y fiestas más autóctonas (por ser de origen ancestral). Generalmente en el baile de yumari, ademas de la cruz o cruces (no de origen cristiano); y el sitio de las ofrendas, colocan otra cruz para los matachines. Parece que en su mentalidad simbólica, la presencia de los matachines es su forma de cristianizar el rito.

La danza de los matachines parece que tiene su origen en el Norte de Italia, en Comélico Superior, Provincia de Venecia, casi lindando con el Tirol Austriaco, en donde, hasta la fecha, practican esa danza en las fiestas del carnaval. El traje es basicamente el mismo, aunque aquí con materiales más modestos. El nombre allá es igual: Matazin. Usan algunas máscaras de madera, como también aqui lo hacen quienes dirigen la danza, los Chapeyones. (Cfr. Ianniello, Cristina, Mondo Ladino XII (1988) 1-4, 11 Carnavale a Comelico Superiore.)

Semana Santa

Actualmente la principal celebración de los Rarámuri Pagótuame son las fiestas de Semana Santa, noríroacbi cuando se dan vueltas -, durante las cuales suelen poner arcos de ramas de pino, que señalan el camino de las múitiples vueltas en procesión de estas festividades. Originariamente se las enseñaron los misioneros, tratando de escenificar pasajes evangélicos de la Semana Mayor. Estas representaciones fueron de tal agrado de los indigenas que atraian multitudes de ellos, como relatan con gran complacencia los antiguos misioneros, pues dichas ceremonias tuvieron gran aceptación entre los indigenas de toda la región. En todas partes donde hay templo se celebran siguiendo basicamente el mismo patrón, aunque con diferencias y adaptaciones propias de cada lugar, como puede comprobarse hasta la fecha, no obstante que no hayan tenido la presencia del Sacerdote durante años. En realidad empiezan el dia de la Candelaria - 2 de febrero - con el uso del tambor, que tocan exclusivamente durante la cuaresma, y el nombramiento de los fariseos en gran número. Gran parte del pueblo participa.

En estas fiestas de Semana Santa participan principalmente dos grupos: el de los fariseos y el de los soldados; ambos tienen sus capitanes que los dirigen; el de los soldados lleva bandera roja y el de los fariseos blanca. (En algunos pueblos hay otros grupos: como el de los pintos en Norogachi; el de los mulatos, con la cara pintada de negro, en Tónachi; el de los moros en Samachiki). Además participan las tenanches, que se encargan de llevar en procesión las imágenes de los santos y de incensar. Y por último los pascoteros, que llevan a cabo la alegre danza del pascol el último dia de la fiesta, con casabeles alrededor de los tobillos y al son de la música de violines y flautas.

Para nosotros, los no indigenas, las ceremonias de Semana Santa de los Rarámuri son las más dificiles de entender porque, aunque fueron aceptadas desde un principio con gran regocijo y agrado de los indigenas, a la partida de los Jesuitas, y al quedarse solos, desde el punto de vista religioso, siguieron celebrando estas fiestas, que habian asumido ya como propias, pero poco a poco fueron olvidando el mito y llenándolas del simbolismo de su propia historia, paralelamente a lo que los españoles hicieron con la escenificación de sus luchas entre moros y cristianos. Los Rarámuri, de una manera admirablemente uniforme en toda la región, simbolizaron a los 'chabochis' en el grupo de los malos,' 'los fariseos,' que se pintan de blanco para representar a los 'chabochi.' Estos son los partidarios de Judas, que en la danza simbólicamente andan en todas partes y dominan la situación, pero que finalmente son vencidos por los soldados o grupo que representa el bien y al final triunfa.

El judas es una figura importante de estas festividades. Suele ser un muñeco hecho de paja, vestido siempre como chabochi, con genitales desmesurados, de quien todos se mofan y al final matan, ya sea quemándolo, fusilandolo o tirándole flechas. En ocasiones, como en Creel y otras partes, le ponen cartas buriescas, en que manifiestan todas las tropelias que sufren de sus opresores y explotadores, descargando asi toda su saña contra ellos en aquel monigote, R. Robles dice muy atinadamente (Ibid): "La Semana Santa es impresionante porque manifiesta el rechazo del proyecto chabochi de una manera ritual pero brutal."

Los pascoleros de Samachiki usan un simbolismo muy significativo de la Resurrección. Después de danzar durante varias horas en la mañana del sabado de la Semana Mayor, ya cerca del mediodia, a la hora de repicar las campanas abriendo la gloria, uno de los pascoleros libera dentro del templo un pajarito, el chuyépari o saltapared, que trae dentro de un canastito colgado del cinturón. Acto seguido viene la muerte de los fariseos, revolcándose estos en el templo y sonando sus espadas de madera en el piso, hasta salir despavoridos aullando; corren luego alrededor del templo, tumbando los arcos del viacrucis y quitándose las plumas con que se habian adornado. En seguida viene la matanza del judas y las luchas entre fariseos y soldados.

Cargos u Oficios

Los antiguos misioneros trataron de concentrar a los indigenas en pueblos para facilitar la comunicación con ellos, pero lo único que se logró fue que sus reuniones las hicieran alrededor del templo, a cuyo lugar los indigenas llaman el pueblo. Al organizarlos asi tuvieron también gran influencia en instaurar los cargos y oficios que actualmente existen en las comunidades indigenas Rarámuri. El principal de estos cargos es el de Gobernador, siriame o jefe de la comunidad y su pastor espiritual; también es el juez en los conflictos, donde más que imponer una sanción, se dirimen las dificultades en forma tranquila y dando consejo para que se restablezca la paz y la armonia en la comunidad. Los siriames son elegidos por acuerdo común y siempre escogen al más probo y prestigiado de la comunidad. Ellos no orientan siguiendo sus propios criterios, sino conforme al mismo consenso de la comunidad.

No sabemos si a la partida de los Misioneros jesuitas, estos delegaron algunos oficios, como los de bautizar, casar, dirigir las reuniones del templo, etc., pues existe muy poca documentación al respecto, ya que los archivos que existian, trataron de enviarse al convento franciscano de Guadalupe, Zacatecas, y nunca llegaron a su destino; sólo existen las cartas que anteriormente habian sido enviadas a la casa provincial de los jesuitas, en México (ahora en el archivo de la Nación en la misma ciudad y en los archivos de Parral) y a la casa generalicia de Roma. El hecho es que, los Rarámuri asumieron, ya sea por encargo o por propia cuenta, algunos oficios que ejercian los Padres Misioneros como el de casar a los contrayentes de nupcias, y otros ritos que pueden equivaler al bautismo que recibian de los misioneros, - o bien este rito ya lo ejercitaban antes en alguna forma y por ello el bautismo encajó tan armoniosamente en su cultura -, el reunirse a rezar en el templo y, sobre todo, el instruir y "pastorear" al pueblo los siriames, o Gobernadores, con sus asiduos nawésaris o sermones, que invariablemente dirigen a su gente enseñando, aconsejando y dirigiendo al pueblo. Transmitiendo asi sus enseñanzas, su teologia, su moral y sus tradiciones.

A fin de cumplir con su oficio, el siriame cuenta con múltiples subordinados, generales, capitanes, mayoras, alguaciles, chapeyones, abanderados, tenanches, resanderos, mayordomos, etc., estos oficios (que pueden variar de un pueblo a otro) son conferidos por el siriame siempre con la aceptación del interesado y del pueblo. Todos estos cargos son de servicio y no de poder o de lucro, pues no reciben por ellos ninguna retribución económica, pero si dan prestigio a quienes los desempeñan. No se ejercen por un tiempo previamente determinado, sino que duran mientras la comunidad está conforme con la forma de desempeñarlo. (Robles, R. Ibid.)

Entre los Rarámuri, el Sacerdote es considerado también como alguien que tiene un cargo de los que ellos designan, el rol de quien puede aconsejar a cualquiera de ellos, incluyendo al siriame. Es quien bautiza, casa en ocasiones, (ya que ellos tienen sus ritos y ministros propios), hace cabeza en las ceremonias del templo, celebra la misa, es perito en las cosas de Dios y las habla de El.

Algo parecido es el oficio que entre ellos ejerce el curandero u owirúame, que es el principal personaje de las ceremonias de enfermedad, vida o muerte, y juega un papel muy importante en la vida de todo Rarámuri, ya que cada uno cuenta con su owirúame, bajo cuya custodia son puestos desde pequeños. - "Estos sacerdotes-doctores tienen sus especialidades. Algunos cantan sólo en las danzas del rutuburi o yúmari, otros únicamente en las fiestas del jiculi ..., otros sólo se dedican a curar ... Todos ayunan y oran concienzudamente, obedeciendo la voluntad de los dioses (?), que imponen restricciones y abstinencia, y por ello se les llama "'owirúami - hombres rectos -. Son los sabios de la tribu, los que hacen llover, los que curan y conservan la herencia común de conocimientos y tradiciones que les presta poderosa influencia sobre los demas" (Lumholtz C. p. 306).

Cultura Diferente no Inferior

Esta breve semblanza de algunas vivencias y esbozo de algunos aspectos de la cultura Rarámuri, nos muestra claramente que su cultura es totalmente diferente pero no por ello inferior, sino simplemente diferente a la nuestra, con una "belleza de relaciones humanas" (como dice Collier), y llena de enseñanzas para nosotros. - Lumholtz abunda: "Es una fortuna que los tarahumaras no hayan sido borrados de la existencia.... Bien puede transcurrir un siglo todavia antes de que todos lleguen a estar al servicio de los blancos o desaparezcan."..."Las futuras generaciones no encontrarán otros recuerdos de los tarahumaras que los que logren recoger los cientificos de hoy, de labios mismos de ese pueblo y del estudio de sus utensilios y costumbres. Han llegado hasta nosotros como restos interesantes de remotas edades, como representantes de una de las etapas de mayor importancia en el desarrollo de la raza humana, como ejemplo de una de aquellas." (p. 410)

Me parece oportuno citar aqui, para concluir este breve ensayo, las palabras de un jóven italiano, Luigi Fabbris, que colaboró aqui en la Misión, entre los indigenas, y últimamente me escribe: ". . . Los Rarámuri tienen mucho que enseñar, saben luchar por la vida y la supervivencia, ojalá que nunca se averguencen de ser indigenas sino que se sientan seguros en su ambiente. Pero si les quitan las tierras y les comen el maiz, si se les hace psicodependientes, sin autonomia, sin libertad, sin conciencia propia, no podrán realizar su modelo cultural. Sin Tarahumaras la humanidad será más pobre. El modelo Tarahumara es la humanidad misma, es la voz de los siglos y los milenios. No son ellos los bárbaros, son un mensaje de poesia y de salvación para nosotros los bárbaros y saqueadores. Extinguirlos o hacerlos desaparecer es suicidio para nosotros. Sin ellos desaparecen unos profetas de la paz, de la tranquilidad, de la parsimonia y de la simbiosis con la naturaleza. Son un mensaje de salvación para nuestra existencia supuestamente civilizada. No dejemos caer en el vacio su voz libertadora. Por eso es que más adelante yo debo volver por alli, a escuchar la voz de esos Juanes Bautista, los Rarámuri."

"El Chamizal" Tourist Information Center

First stop across the border
Av. de las Americas #2551
Cd. Juárez, Chih.

Toll Free From U.S.A.
1-888-654-0394
(16) 11-3174

1 Puente Santa Fe Santa Fe Bridge
2 Centro de Información Turística "El Chamizal" "El Chamizal" Tourist Information Center
3 Puente Libre de Córdova o de las Americas Cordova or America's Free Bridge

Tourist Information

Government Palace
Downtown Chihuahua City
Av. Carranza y Aldama
Chihuahua, Chih.

Toll Free
01-800 849-5200
(1) 429-36421

NOMBRE	TEL.	FAX	CORREO ELECTRONICO
Copper Canyon Adventures	415-7230	416-0900	
Ch-P Tours	437-0057	437-0058	Chptours@buzon.online.com.mx
Divitur	414-6046	421-1676	Divitur@hotmail.com
Ferromex	410-3751	415-7756	edominguez@ferromex.com.mx
Linusa	410-0000	415-8930	Linusa@chih1.uninet.net.mx
México by Train	413-9020	414-6690	
Rojo y Casavantes	415-5858	415-5384	Rycsa@chih1.uninet.net.mx
Sierra Madre Tours	418-2516	411-3706	
South Orient Express	410-7570	800-6597602	Trainsoe@infosel.net.mx
Sportsman's Travel	410-5030	888-3130152	Elhalcon@chihuahua.podernet.com.mx
Tara Adventures	417-3804		
Turismo al Mar	410-9232	416-6589	Turmar@chih1.telmex.net.mx
Vía Cobre	415-1199	415-6575	Hoteldivisadero@infosel.net.mx
Viajes Siglo XXI	426-6464	414-5224	
Viajes Dorados	414-6438	414-6490	Mextour@infosel.net.mx

CITY / HOTEL	ADDRESS	PHONE	FAX	# ROOMS
CHIHUAHUA CITY (14)				
HOTEL WESTIN SOBERANO	BARRANCA DEL COBRE 3211	29-2929	29-2900	204
HOLIDAY INN HOTEL & SUITES	ESCUDERO 702	14-3350	14-3313	74
HOTEL SAN FRANCISCO	VICTORIA 409	16-7550 / 16-7770	15-3538	131
HOTEL CASA GRANDE	TECNOLOGICO 4702	39-4444	39-4448	115
HOTEL FIESTA INN	BLVD. ORTIZ MENA 2801	29-0100	29-0110	152
HOTEL PALACIO DEL SOL	INDEPENDENCIA 500	16-6000	15-9947	183
HOTEL SICOMORO	BLVD. ORTIZ MENA 411	13-5445	13-1411	128
HOTEL CENTRAL PALACE	PRIV. GRAL. ROBERTO FIERRO 8017	29-1929	29-1929	72
MOTEL BEST WESTERN MIRADOR	UNIVERSIDAD 1309	13-2205	13-8906	87
MOTEL PARADOR SAN MIGUEL	TECNOLOGICO 7901-23	17-0303	17-1500	44
HOTEL SAN AGUSTIN	ALLENDE 504	10-7152 / 10-7919	10-79-19	58
MOTEL POSADA TIERRA BLANCA	NIÑOS HEROES 102	15-0000	16-0063	106
HOTEL MARROD	TECNOLOGICO 10111	19-4611 / 19-0323	19-4611 / 19-0323	56
HOTEL PARADOR CHIHUAHUA	CALLE 3a. 304	15-0827	15-0829	28
HOTEL APOLO	JUAREZ 907	16-1101 / 16-1100	16-1102	44
HOTEL EL CAMPANARIO	BLVD. DIAZ ORDAZ Y PRIV. DE LIBERTAD	15-4545 / 15-4979	15-4214	30
HOTEL EL DORADO DAYS INN	CALLE 14 #321	10-2227 / 10-2228	15-5932	58
HOTEL AVENIDA	JUARES Y V. CARRANZA 1101	15-2891	15-2891	56
SUITE DEL REY INN	LAZARD DE BAIGORRI 601	14-5888 / 14-0027	14-5888 / 14-0027	8
MOTEL BALFLO	ALDAMA Y 21a.	15-4340	55	
HOTEL SAN JUAN	VICTORIA 823	10-0035	10-0035	60
NUEVO CASAS GRANDES (169)				
HOTEL HACIENDA	AVE. BENITO JUAREZ 2603	4-1046 / 4-1047	4-48-18	124
HOTEL LAS FUENTES	AVE. COLON S/N	4-5402 / 4-5410	4-0712	56
HOTEL CALIFORNIA	AVE. CONSTITUCION 209	4-2214 / 4-1110	40	
HOTEL PAQUIME	AVE. BENITO JUAREZ 401	4-1320 / 4-4720	4-47-20	45
MOTEL PIÑON	AVE. BENITO JUAREZ 605	4-0655 / 4-0166	4-1705	57
MOTEL LOS ARCOS	CARR. NVO. CASAS GRANDES-CHIH.	4-42-60	4-42-60	29
HOTEL JUAREZ	OBREGON NO. 110	4-0233	36	
R.V. PARK LOS ARCOS	CARR. NVO. CASAS GRANDES-CHIH.	4-42-60	4-42-60	25
MADERA (157)				
MOTEL REAL DEL BOSQUE	AVE. CHIHUAHUA S/N	2-0538	2-0066	25
PARADOR DE LA SIERRA	CALLE 3ª E INDEPENDENCIA	2-0277	2-0785	20
HOSTAL PRESA PEÑITAS	CALLE 4A. #1103	10-1077 / (157) 2-0	10-1077 / (157) 2-0	12
HOTEL MIRMAY	CALLE 3ª Y GUERRERO	2-0944	14	
CIUDAD JUAREZ (16)				
HOTEL CASA GRANDE	AV. TECNOLOGICO 3620	29-4046	29-4000	145
HOTEL LUCERNA	PASEO TRIUNFO DE LA REP. 3976	29-9900 / 13-3778	13-2600	138
HOTEL PLAZA JUAREZ	AV. LINCOLN Y COYOACAN	13-1310	13-0084	175
HOTEL SUITES EL PASEO	PASEO TRIUNFO DE LA REP. 4850	11-50-00	11-50-00	106
HOLIDAY INN	PASEO TRIUNFO DE LA REP. 3747	29-6000	29-6020	148
COLONIAL	AV. LINCOLN Y AV. AMERICAS 1355	13-5050	13-4081	229
MARIA BONITA (SUITES)	AV. RAFAEL PEREZ SERNA 1721	27-0303	27-0767	45
VILLA DEL SOL	PASEO TRIUNFO DE LA REP. 339 SUR	17-2624	17-3030	118
MAR CHULAVISTA	PASEO TRIUNFO DE LA REP. 3555	17-1207	18-6288	140
DELUXE	AV. LERDO Y GALEANA 300	15-0082	15-0082	68
CONTINENTAL	AV. LERDO 112 SUR	15-0084	14-0531	65
IMPALA	AV. LERDO 670 NORTE	15-0491	15-0431	38
SANTA FE	AV. LERDO Y TLAXCALA 290	15-1560	14-0382	80
MONACO	PASEO TRIUNFO DE LA REP. 3335	16-1677	16-3154	108
LA TEJA	PASEO TRIUNFO DE LA REP. 4817	16-6999	13-2479	76
VILLA MANPORT	AV. HERMANOS ESCOBAR 2224	16-4888	16-2394	56
PLAZA CONSULADO	AV. LOPEZ MATEOS 1120	11-48-84	11-48-85	77
MONTECARLO	PASEO TRIUNFO DE LA REP. 6310	17-7938	17-1201	83
INTERNAC. LA PLAYA	AV. LOPEZ MATEOS 1035 NTE.	13-71-87	11-44-08	117
CAMARGO (146)				
SANTA FE	CARR. PANAMERICANA KM. 67.5	2-40-22	2-41-42	64
LOS NOGALES	AV. JUAREZ 404	2-1247	2-44-42	52
JIMENEZ (154)				
LAS PAMPAS	CARR. JIMENEZ-CHIHUAHUA .960	2-1041	2-1610	42
FLORIDO	AV. JUAREZ Y 20 DE NOVIEMBRE	2-0400	7	

CITY / HOTEL	ADDRESS	PHONE	FAX	# ROOMS
HIDALGO DEL PARRAL (152)				
ADRIANA	C. COLEGIO #2	2-25-70	2-47-70	62
MILLER INN	CARR. A DURANGO ENT. CON PERIFERICO	3-0335	3-0330	58
LOS ARCOS	PEDRO DE LILLE #13	3-0597	3-0537	38
MOREIRA	MACLOVIO HERRERA 79	2-1710	40	
CAMINO REAL	INDEPENDENCIA S/N	3-0202	3-0262	85
TURISTA	PLAZA INDEPENDENCIA 12	3-40-70	3-40-70	40
BASASEACHI (1)				
ALMA ROSA	HOTEL	(145) 6-0397	10	
VILLA ALPINA	CABIN	15-2222	9	
RANCHO SAN LORENZO	CABIN / CAMPING & RV	414-6046	421-1676	5
CREEL (145)				
BEST WESTERN LODGE	HOTEL	6-0071	6-0082	18
CASCADA INN	MOTEL	6-0253	6-0151	32
PARADOR DE LA MONTAÑA	MOTEL	6-0075	6-0075	48
NUEVO BARRANCAS DEL COBRE	MOTEL	6-0022	28	
PLAZA MEXICANA	HOTEL	6-0245	26	
KORACHI	HOTEL	6-0207	22	
BERTIS	CABIN	6-0086	10	
POSADA DE CREEL	BED & BREAKFAST	6-0142	6-0262	21
HOSTAL CUEVA DE LOS LEONES	CABIN	(14) 10-1077	(14) 10-1077	12
CABAÑAS MILEDY	CABIN	6-0069	4	
CABAÑAS MONTEBELLO	CABIN	(14) 23-0643	(14) 23-0643	3
MARGARITAS	BED & BREAKFAST	6-0045	41	
ARAREKO (145)				
SEGORACHI	CABIN	6-0126	1	
BATOSARACHI	BED & BREAKFAST	6-0126	3	
CUZARARE (1)				
CAÑON DEL COBRE	LODGE	414-8715	414-8716	23
EL TEJABAN (146)				
TEJABAN	HOTEL	2-1247	21	
BATOPILAS				
RIVERSIDE LODGE	HOTEL	(1) 414-8715	(1)414-8716	15
CASA REAL DE MINAS	HOTEL	(145) 6-0624	7	
MARY	HOTEL	(145) 6-0624	10	
JUANITA	HOTEL	(145) 6-0624	9	
CASA MONSE	HOTEL	(145) 6-0624	8	
BATOPILAS	HOTEL	(145) 6-0624	8	
PALMERAS	HOTEL	(145) 6-0624	8	
CLARITA	HOTEL	(145) 6-0624	10	
CHULA VISTA	HOTEL	(145) 6-0624	8	
HOTEL MARGARITAS	HOTEL	(145) 6-0045	14	
CASA FIGUEROA	HOTEL	(145) 6-0624	5	
DIVISADERO				
POSADA BARRANCAS MIRADOR	HOTEL	(68) 18-7046	(68) 12-0046	32
POSADA BARRANCAS RANCHO	HOTEL	(68) 18-7046	(68) 12-0046	36
DIVISADERO BARRANCAS	HOTEL	415-1199	415-6575	52
MANSION TARAHUMARA	HOTEL	415-4721	416-5444	45
HOSTAL OTEVIACHI	CABIN	10-1077 / (145) 6-4	(14) 10-1077	9
HOSTAL GUITAYVO	CABIN	10-1077 / (145) 6-4	(14) 10-1077	6
CEROCAHUI (1)				
MISION	HOTEL	(68) 18-7046	(68) 12-0046	34
PARAISO DEL OSO	HOTEL	421-3372	421-3372	21
MARGARITAS	LODGE	(145) 6-0245	(145) 6-0075	6
CABAÑAS CAÑON DE URIQUE	CABIN	423-1820	12	
GUACHOCHI (154)				
MELINA	HOTEL	3-0255	3-0340	46
CHAPARRO	HOTEL	3-0005	25	
DELICIAS (14)				
CASA GRANDE	74-0404	74-0405	73	
PARAISO DORADO	73-1050	60		
BAEZA	72-1000	48		
DEL NORTE	72-0200	72-0200	25	
OTACHIQUE, MPIO. DE URUACHI				
HOSTAL OTACHIQUE	CABIN	10-1077 / (145) 6-0	10-1077 / (145) 6-0	12

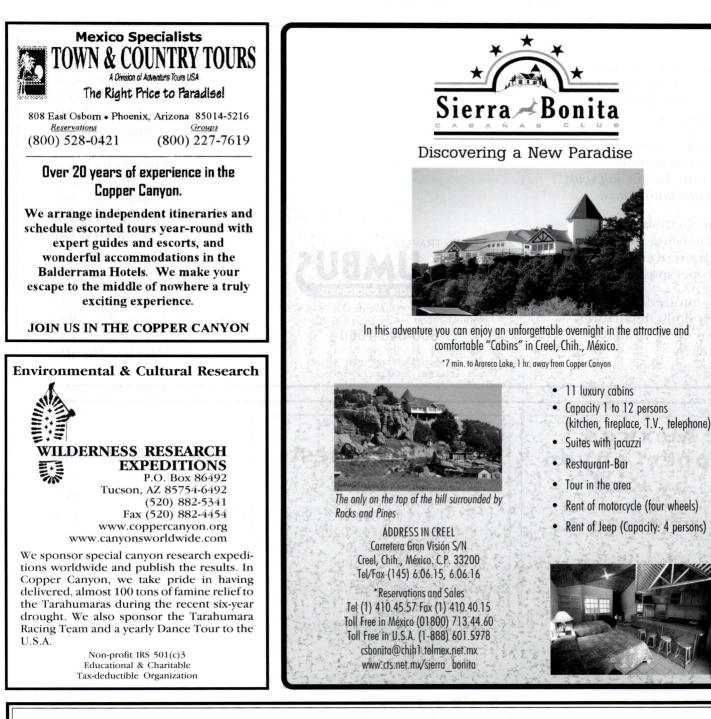

Basic Travel Tips for Copper Canyon

To obtain a visa, the traveler must have a proof of citizenship which may be a passport, birth certificate, voter's registration or draft card. A complete Spanish-English dictionary is highly recommended. Automobile insurance and visas are mandatory.

In recent years Mexico has had various credit card only fees and deposits on private vehicles driven into Mexico on tourist visas. These change from time-to-time so be prepared.

Water — As with all travel outside the U.S. and worldwide, *all* water must be boiled for safety. Recommended is bringing five to ten-gallons of drinking water *only* and a separate, refillable jug for washing and cooking purposes.

Food — With the exception of major towns, food is generally limited to eggs, range-fed beef, tortillas, beans, potatoes, coffee and soda pop. These items can be obtained just about anywhere.

Gas — Only major cities have "extra" gas (about 85 octane). In the mountains *Nova* (very poor regular gas) is available at infrequent intervals. Fill the tank at every opportunity and keep a 5-10 gallon reserve in cans. Poor quality gas is probably the worst problem encountered in visiting the parks.

Tires — Recommended are five new tires and an excellent spare.

General Travel Advice — Everything in this book is in the best Spanish tradition, *alineamiento aproximado*, and in the best English tradition, "subject to change without notice," so keep your thinking cap on at all times, talk to everyone you meet, ask questions, and have the greatest adventure of your life!

Extensive travel in Mexico and South America has shown that one can survive on a vocabulary of less than 200 Spanish words. Here are the most important words and phrases for travel in northwest Mexico.

please - por favor	beans - frijoles	five - cinco
where is? - ¿donde está?	bread - tortillas	six - seis
road (or trail) - camino	potatoes - papas	seven - siete
town - pueblo	auto oil - aceite	eight - ocho
hotel - hotel	gas - gasolina	nine - nueve
restaurant - restaurante	ice - hielo	ten - diez
house - casa	water - agua	twenty - viente
falls - cascada	more - mas	thirty - treinta
canyon - barranca	very hot - mucho calor	forty - cuarenta
mountains - montañas	very cold - mucho frio	fifty - cincuenta
(sierra)	pretty - bonita	sixty - sesenta
high - alto	Indians - indigenista	seventy - setenta
low - abajo	why - ¿por qué?	eighty - ochenta
store - tienda	what - ¿qué?	ninety - noventa
let's go - ¡vámanos!	where - ¿donde?	one hundred - ciento
river - río	when - cuando	one thousand - mil
meal - comida	who - ¿quién?	
north - norte	much - mucho	
south - sur	thank you - gracias	
east - este	you're welcome - por nada	
west - oeste	How much does this	
lake - laguna/lago	cost? - ¿Cuánto cuesta?	
mission - misión	bathroon - baño	
you - usted		
we - nosotros	**Numbers**	
I want - Yo quiero	one - uno	
I would like - Me gustaría	two - dos	
meat - carne	three - tres	
eggs - huevos	four - cuatro	

Weights and Measures

U.S. - Metric

Distance

U.S.		Metric
1 mi	-	1.61 km
5 mi	-	8.05 km
10 mi	-	16.09 km
30 mi	-	48.27 km
50 mi	-	80.45 km
80 mi	-	128.72 km
100 mi	-	160.9 km

U.S. - Metric

Length

U.S.		Metric
1 in	-	2.54 cm
5 in	-	12.7 cm
10 in	-	25.4 cm
1 yd	-	0.914 m
5 yd	-	4.57 m
10 yd	-	9.14 m

Weight

1 oz	-	28 g
5 oz	-	142 g
10 oz	-	283 g
1 lb	-	0.45 kg
5 lb	-	2.25 kg
10 lb	-	4.5 kg

Capacity

ounce	-	.0296 l
pint (16 oz)	-	.4739 l
quart (32 oz)	-	.9463 l
gallon (4 qt)	-	3.78 l
10 gallons	-	37.8 l

Temperature

Fahrenheit	-	Celsius
100°	-	38.5°
80°	-	26.5°
32°	-	0°
0°	-	-17.8°

Bibliography

Sierra Madre

Unknown Mexico, Carl Lumholtz, M.A. Charles Scribner's Sons, New York, 1902.

Chihuahua: A Guide to the Wonderful Country, Richard H. Hancock, University of Oklahoma Press, 1978.

Mexico's Copper Canyon Country - A Hiking and Backpacking Guide to Tarahumara Land, M. John Fayhee, Cordillera Press, Inc., P.O. Box 3699, Evergreen, CO 80439, $12.95, 1989.

Native Americans

Cycles of Conquest, Edward H. Spicer, The University of Arizona Press, Tucson, AZ, 1962.

Rarámuri, A Tarahumara Colonial Chronicle 1607-1791, Thomas E. Sheridan and Thomas H. Naylor, editors, Northland Press, Flagstaff, AZ, 1979.

Tarahumara of Mexico: Their Environment and Material Culture, Campbell W. Pennington, The University of Utah Press, Salt Lake City, 1963.

Tarahumara - Where Night Is the Day of the Moon, Bernard L. Fontana with photography by John P. Schaefer, Northland Press, Flagstaff, AZ, 1979.

People of the Desert and Sea - Ethnobotany of the Seri Indians, Richard S. Felger and Mary Beck Moser, University of Arizona Press, Tucson, AZ, 1985.

Semana Santa in the Sierra Tarahumara: A Comparative Study of Three Communities, John C. Kennedy and Raul A. Lopez, University of California Press, Berkeley and Los Angeles, 1981.

Missions — Sierra Madre

Spanish Jesuit Churches in Mexico's Tarahumara, Paul M. Roca, University of Arizona Press, Tucson, AZ, 1979.

Earlier Jesuit Missions in Tarahumara, Peter Master Dunne, S.J., University of California Press, Berkeley and Los Angeles, 1948.

Railroad

Destination Topolobampo, John Leeds Kerr with Frank Donovan, Golden West Books, San Marino, CA, 1968.

Rails, Mines and Progress: Seven American Promoters in Mexico 1867-1911, David M. Pletcher, American Historical Association, Cornell University Press, 1958 (also Batopilas and Mexico general).

Flora

Biotic Community of the American Southwest - United States and Mexico, David E. Brown, Editor, University of Arizona Press for the Boyce Thompson Southwestern Arboretum, P.O. Box AB, Superior, AZ, 1982.

Fauna

The Grizzly in the Southwest, Documentary of Extinction, David E. Brown, University of Oklahoma Press, Norman 1985.

The Wolf in the Southwest, David E. Brown, University of Arizona Press, Tucson, AZ, 1963.

Harper and Row's Complete Field Guide to North American Wildlife (Western Edition), Harper and Row Publishers, New York, 1981.

A Field Guide to Mexican Birds, Rober Tory Peterson, Edward L. Chalif, (Audubon Society and National Wildlife Federation) Houghton Mifflin Company, Boston, 1973.

Baja

The Magnificent Peninsula, Jack Williams, H.J. Williams, P.O. Box 203, Sausalito, CA, 1986.

Camping and Climbing in Baja, John W. Robinson, La Siesta Press, Box 406, Glendale, CA, 1983.

Mexico - Culture - History

Mexico, Kal Muller and Guillermo García-Oropeza, Insight Guides, APA Productions Prentice Hall, Harrap Lansdowne, 1984.